BOOKS of FAITH and POWER

Books of

FAITH and POWER

By
JOHN T. McNEILL

Essay Index Reprint Series

BOOKS FOR LIBRARIES PRESS
FREEPORT, NEW YORK

INTERNATIONAL STANDARD BOOK NUMBER:
0-8369-1996-3

LIBRARY OF CONGRESS CATALOG CARD NUMBER:
75-134112

PRINTED IN THE UNITED STATES OF AMERICA

CONTENTS

FOREWORD

Great books, even the greatest, would be neglected by many of those who ought to read them if they were not from time to time brought to notice in slighter and more ephemeral ones. The six that are reviewed in the following chapters may justly claim a prominent place among those which express basic elements of the Christian tradition. It is my hope that these pages will arouse in some readers unacquainted with the originals an impulse to study them. Perhaps, also, readers who already know some or all of these "books of faith and power" will find it useful to compare their judgments of them with the impressions here conveyed.

The materials of the first three and the last of the series were substantially contained in four lectures delivered during the month of January, 1945, in the Jewish Theological Seminary of America, New York City, under the auspices of the Institute for Religious Studies. These lectures formed part of a triple series entitled "Classics of Western Religion," in which other lecturers presented Roman Catholic and Jewish works of similar distinction. Within the larger series the four here included were announced under the special designation, "Protestant Classics." These discourses have been revised and enlarged, and in this process marks of the lecture form have been eliminated. The book has been extended to include treatments of *The Pilgrim's Progress* and the *Serious Call*. What is attempted, in each chapter except the last, is a digest aided by a few quotations and interspersed with interpretative comment. Since Wesley's *Journal* could not usefully be reduced to an outline, I have sought to characterize it chiefly by means of extracts grouped to illustrate topics of special interest. Only a minimum necessary attention is given to the lives of the authors.

The selection of titles has been made with a view to variety of material rather than with purpose to secure the cumulative effect of a series of similar writings. While all have in common a body of Christian teaching, they differ widely in content and expression. Luther gives eager utterance to his fresh discovery of a faith that yields service in freedom; Calvin builds a theology from Scripture materials around the theme of the sovereign majesty and unmerited grace of God; Hooker is the philosophical theologian, willing to submit all to the tests of reason; Bunyan transports us to a world of vivid imagery where the faithful triumph after much tribulation; Law hurls a challenge to the ungodly and pleads for a resolute and ordered devotion; and Wesley, while himself no stranger in this brilliant company, is the honest reporter of a career of unique religious activity.

JOHN T. McNEILL

July 1, 1947

NOTE FOR THE
"BOOKS FOR LIBRARIES" REPRINT

I take pleasure in greeting a new generation of readers for this volume. Each of the works examined in these elementary essays has its own specific importance in the Christian tradition. Today's religious experience and discussion may affect the interpretation of such writings, and some readers may find reason to offer their own improvements on my treatment. The happiest result of an acquaintance with what I have said here would be that the reader should search the works themselves and become his own interpreter. I am sincerely grateful to the Publishers for selecting this book for membership in the "Books for Libraries" series, and to Mrs. Beverly Bass for permitting me, in their behalf, to insert this note.

JOHN T. MCNEILL

Middlebury, Vermont
September 28, 1970

MARTIN LUTHER
On Christian Liberty

Chapter I

MARTIN LUTHER:

On Christian Liberty

MEN comparable to Martin Luther in sheer historic eminence do not appear in every century. He came to manhood in an age ripe for change and he was endowed with high gifts of leadership. Circumstances and personality combined to make him the chief agent of a transformation of Western Christianity that has profoundly affected modern civilization. His role in this vast upheaval was rendered possible by a prior conflict fought out to a decision in the depth of his own soul. Through long inward agony he had come to a glad moment of deliverance and thereby had become possessed of resources for a lifetime of outward striving. In the quiet of a small university, and with little thought at first of the epochal importance of his new insight for the world, he entered upon the task of shaping a theology consonant with this experience. But a few years later, confronted by the challenge of a gross abuse, he was constrained to break into the open with his Ninety-five Theses against indulgences. He could not then foresee what was to follow; but from this utterance the outward battle began for which his inward victory had prepared him. At an early stage in the controversy he paused to write the immortal book which is his best attempt to convey to others the fruits of his personal experience, the *Treatise on Christian Liberty*. The nature of this experience, and the con-

3

victions to which it led, will be more closely observed as we proceed.

The book was written in October and published in November, 1520. It appeared in Latin and in German: the Latin was apparently the original although the somewhat shorter German edition was off the press a few days before it. Christianity had produced many cherished books before Luther's time, but this is the earliest that can properly be designated as a representative Protestant classic. When we compare with it the Reformer's slightly earlier treatises, we realize that, historically significant as these are, they contain less that is of central importance and of timeless value. The more noteworthy of these preceding and related writings of Luther claim at the outset a brief notice, that we may see our little book in its setting.

In the three years that had elapsed since the publication of the theses on indulgences Luther had been heavily engaged in controversy, and under the pressure of a variety of attacks had been thinking his way onward. His debate with John Eck at Leipzig early in July, 1519, had convinced him that he stood in danger of excommunication from the papal church and set him to the rethinking, and the defense, of his position. Since this disputation he had already written numerous short treatises. The *Tessaradecas Consolatoria* (Fourteen of Consolation) appeared in September, 1519. It is a work of warm piety, artificially constructed around fourteen patron saints, and was written for the spiritual guidance of the elector of Saxony, who at the time was seriously ill. It exalts the Church as the communion of saints, and at its close contains anticipations of the main argument of the tract *On Christian Liberty*.

Four of Luther's writings of 1520 exhibit further the fruits of his developing thought. The *Treatise on Good Works* occupied much of his time in the spring months of that year and was published about the beginning of June. It was written to correct the error, fostered by his opponents, that in urging the primacy of faith he had intended to forbid good works. The thought is developed by means of an interpretation of the Ten Commandments as the divine plan of good works. Of these the First Commandment, because it enjoins faith in the true God, is called "the highest and best, from which all the others flow." Boehmer's view that this treatise is superior to *On Christian Liberty* can be upheld only on the ground of the more systematic method of argument which it exhibits. In large degree, it is true, Luther here anticipates the positions taken in the more vital tract which we are about to examine, and the treatise contains some brilliant gems of spiritual insight. But for the most part we miss in it the zest and energy, springing from a complete emancipation of the writer's soul, that find expression in *On Christian Liberty*

Also in June of that year appeared *On the Papacy at Rome*. It was an answer to a Franciscan named Augustin Alveld who had attacked Luther with bitter invective. Luther is equally caustic and vituperative in his reply. Admitting that his words are "barbed with scorn," he begs his readers to believe that his heart is breaking with sorrow at his opponent's flippant treatment of Scripture. Though marred by violent language, this treatise has the value of offering, in passages of admirable clarity, an index to Luther's conception of the Church as a spiritual community.

Luther had formally appealed for the meeting of a free general council of the Church, November 18, 1518, and he was to repeat this appeal just two years later. The expectation of reform by means of councils was in his mind when he wrote the *Address to the Christian Nobility of the German Nation*, which was published in August, 1520. This powerful tract begins by assailing the three "walls of straw and paper" by which the papacy attempts to guard its privileges: the exclusive claims of the clergy as the "spiritual estate," the pope's sole authority in the interpretation of Scripture, and his sole right to summon general councils. Luther here affirms the rights of all faithful laymen, as themselves "consecrated priests," each "serving the others by his work or office." He sets forth at length specific demands for a far-reaching reform of the Church, and presents a schedule of measures to be acted upon in reforming councils. Although Luther (like most earlier conciliarists) did not believe in the infallibility of councils, he allowed them a certain authority when they worked in accordance with Scripture. "God help a free council," he exclaims, "to teach the pope that he too is a man." Through long years thereafter he and his followers kept on demanding conciliar action for reform.

Early in October, 1520, came *The Babylonish Captivity of the Church*, a radical discussion of the sacraments. Luther holds that under the papacy the sacraments "have been subjected to a miserable captivity," whereby the Christian people have lost their liberty. He hopes this situation will be ended by action of a general council, and "our Christian liberty restored." He acknowledges baptism and the Eucharist as the two scriptural sacraments and gives an inferior place to penance, while he declines to admit to the rank of sacraments the other four of the accepted seven. His treatment of ordination is typical in its denial of clerical privilege and assertion of the priesthood of all believers. "He who has Christ has all things that are Christ's and is able to do all things." What the priest does in the conduct of worship is done in behalf of all, for all alike possess the priesthood which he is appointed to exercise for them. *On Christian Liberty* may be thought of as culminating this series of utterances. While it is written in a higher tone, and is a more fervently religious book, it contains some materials that have already found lucid expression in the earlier treatises.

The book is also a sequel to the effort of Pope Leo X to end the controversy by obtaining a recantation from Luther. In an interview with Luther in October, 1518, Cardinal Caietanus had failed to secure this. Carl von Miltitz, a Saxon cleric of noble family, who had been at Rome in the service of the Elector Frederick of Saxony, was then employed by the Pope to seek an act of submission from Luther. Luther conferred with him in January, 1519, and thereafter confessed that he had advanced the truth too zealously and was now prepared "to follow the Church of Rome with obedience and respect." He also wrote to the pope a conciliatory letter, which, however, was not delivered. A second meeting with Miltitz took place in October, 1519, and a third a year later. To meet the wishes of Miltitz in this last interview between them, Luther prepared the letter "To Leo the Tenth, Pope at Rome" which serves as introduction to our treatise. This introductory letter shows a change of attitude on Luther's part as compared with the submissive tone of the letter of March, 1519, which had followed his first meeting with Miltitz. Since that time the Leipzig Debate had been held, and the bull *Exsurge Domine*, demanding a simple and complete recantation on pain of excommunication, had been issued. At Miltitz' suggestion the letter to Leo was dated back to September 6, a device to suggest that it was written before the bull reached Saxony. We may suppose, too, that Miltitz expected it to contain concessions which actually it does not contain. It was probably without his prompting, however, that Luther accompanied the letter to the pope with the treatise, which quite outweighs it in bulk and importance. It is not known whether the pope received this double package.

The letter to Pope Leo cannot be dismissed without a
brief indication of its contents. Luther recalls that he has
been compelled to appeal from the pope to a future council: he has, nevertheless, besought God with earnest prayers
for His Blessedness. The pope in the midst of the corruption
of the Curia is a Daniel amid the lions in Babylon. "There
is no hope for the Roman Curia: . . . it hates councils, it fears
reformation."[1] Luther recites argumentatively the history
of his doings with papal protagonists and emissaries. He appeals to Leo to do two things only: to restrain his flatterers
who are enemies of peace, and to admit freedom of interpretation of the Scriptures. He ventures to write because the
pope is in need of "even help from the least of his brethren."
The little treatise is presented as evidence of the kind of
studies Luther would prefer to the controversies thrust upon
him.

It is evident that Luther had been encouraged in this
matter by reading the celebrated work of St. Bernard of
Clairvaux, De Consideratione, a brief treatise written about
the middle of the twelfth century to advise and warn Pope
Eugenius III (1145–53). Twice the letter alludes to this treatise: it is, he says, "a book every pope should have by heart."
Luther does not quote Bernard directly. He may have had
in mind the earnest monk's exhortation to Eugenius: "Reflect that you are a man, naked and poor and wretched
and pitiable . . . a man born for toil and not for honors; a
man born of woman and therefore born in sin. . . . Supreme
Pontiff, and none the less . . . the vilest dust." Luther probably remembered that Leo could also, if he chose, read in
Bernard a warning against the "universal plague" of simony,

[1] Most of the passages here quoted in English are from the translation by W. A. Lambert in *Works of Martin Luther* (Philadelphia: Hol-
man, 1916), II. The Latin quotations are from the Weimar edition of
Luther's *Werke*, in which the *Treatise on Christian Liberty* is in Volume VII.

and a satirical acknowledgment that the wickedness of the Romans could not be cured but only cared for: *"curam exigeris, non curationem,"* runs Bernard's characteristic play on words, and it is appropriately supported by a quotation from Ovid. In Luther's citation of Jeremiah 51:9, *"Curavimus Babylonem et non est sanata"* ("We would have healed Babylon, but she is not healed"), there may lurk a memory of this language of the medieval saint. But Luther, equating Babylon with the papacy, completes the quotation: *"dereliquamus eam"* ("let us forsake her"). Lamenting that the intervening age has brought only an increase of corruption, he uses language more condemnatory than that of Bernard and applies it more directly to the papacy itself. Whereas the Cistercian had affirmed in strong terms a divine-right authority in the papacy, Luther declares that a pope under the influence of flatterers who teach him to think of himself as lord of the world is "Antichrist and an idol." Luther also takes occasion to call the papal champion, John Eck, an enemy of Christ, and to suggest that the cardinals suffer from an incurable spiritual gout, and that the name of the Curia is malodorous throughout the world.

II

The treatise itself is largely free from the animus of controversy. Its basic theme is faith and the fruits of faith. Faith, Luther says, is held to be an easy thing by those who have no experience of it. It can be well explained only by one who has "at some time tested the courage faith gives a man when trials oppress him." As for himself, "driven about by great and various temptations," he has at any rate attained to a little faith.

These opening words all too briefly allude to experiences that made Luther the reformer he was. He had arrived at his faith and inner freedom through anguish of soul. In the ascetic exercises of his order and the penitential system of the medieval Church he failed to find rest and peace. Through all such practices he was haunted by the thought of the incompleteness and defect of penitential satisfaction. He had learned from the Ockhamists that absolutions are not acts of forgiveness unless they are attended by the repentence of perfect love. He had undoubtedly a scrupulous and sensitive conscience, as well as a keen imagination. Fasts, prayers and vigils left him with torturing images of doom and seemed to lead only to deeper involvements. He felt a vast insecurity and at times a sense of abandonment. He was confronted by a demand that he could not meet, and which no multiplication of works could satisfy. There was a hopelessly accumulating deficit of righteousness, or debt to the justice of God. Luther shuddered at the phrase, "justice of God" ("*Justitia Dei*"). "The words 'just' and 'justice,'" he said afterwards, "were a thunderbolt in my conscience." He found no "firm consolation" in the routines of religion as it functioned about him.

Perhaps the fact that he was now (1512) a professor of theology, and needed to give lectures in which his hearers could find light and consistency, hastened and intensified the process of his illumination. He had gained some help from his monastic friend, John Staupitz, from the mystical writings of St. Bernard and those of Jean Gerson, whom he called "Doctor Consolatorius," from the *German Theology*, an anonymous mystical book of the school of John Tauler, and most of all from St. Paul; but he later felt that it was not these intermediaries but God himself who had led him through the darkness and out into the light. Not that he received peculiar revelations. He believed that his experience was normal in the sense that it showed the common way of the working of God's grace. He finally gave up the battle of works and made the venture of faith. He reflected on Romans 1:17: "*Justitia Dei in eo revelatur. . . .*" ("Therein is the righteousness of God revealed . . . the just shall live by faith"). "At last," he says, "I perceived that the justice of God is that by which the just man lives, that is to say faith. . . . Thereupon I felt as if born again. It seemed to me as if heaven's gate stood full open and I was joyfully entering therein." The expression "justice of God" became now no longer terrifying, but "the sweetest of words." It is not that active justice by which the sinner is judged and condemned, but that passive justice which is imputed to the sinner in his need when he has faith. It is God, too, who gives the faith that justifies. All is God's work, not ours. "The righteousness that is in us is from God by faith."

Faith, then, is that by which the just shall live. It is of this treasure of faith that Luther will speak. His is a very personal realization of God's pardoning and enabling grace. By it the soul may know that the righteousness of Christ is made its own righteousness, freeing it from the dominion of sin. Faith is at once the condition of justification and the source of moral renewal—of an unshakable courage and a victorious freedom.

As we saw, the work came out in German and in Latin. The German title is naturally translated: "The Freedom of a Christian Man." The Latin is a little different: "Concerning Christian Liberty." "*Freiheit*" and "*libertas*" are of course intended as equivalents. In English usage a distinction has sometimes been made, in view of certain trends in modern European history, between "freedom" and "liberty." "Freedom" is liberty made secure by the restraints of law, the acknowledgement of obligations, while "liberty" may be unregulated and correspondingly unstable.[2] Luther is not

---

[2] Cf. William Benett, *Freedom and Liberty* (New York: Oxford University Press, 1920).

playing with such a distinction. But if we ask ourselves whether the freedom or liberty of which he writes is something regulated, conditioned and obligated or something unregulated and irresponsible, we find the answer to be very definitely that it is the former. He is presenting an ordered freedom in the personal life, a freedom that is as far from anarchy as from tyranny.

Luther lived in an age when few men spoke enthusiastically about freedom or liberty. Perhaps no one then thought of it so clearly, comprehensively and profoundly as some thinkers of our time have done. When Pope Hildebrand raised the claim of liberty, what he had primarily in mind was the liberty of the hierarchical Church from interference by princes. When the Scottish patriots of 1320 declared that they were fighting for "the freedom which no good man surrenders but with his life," they were thinking mainly of the political ideal of national autonomy. The "liberties of Parliament" in England were certain time-honored privileges of the estates of Parliament; the "Gallican liberties" meant certain claims of independent action, based upon medieval concordats and usages, on the part of the French Church, or on the part of the French state in Church matters. There were also current notions of the liberties of cities that were freeing themselves from feudal lordship. Luther is concerned with no such matters. Nor is he engaged here in the old debate of the theologians about the freedom of the will of man as a problem in anthropology to be treated independently of questions of faith and of salvation. That subject he would take up a few years later in controversy with Erasmus.

III

The reformer's main conception of the twofold effect of faith is flashed upon the reader's mind at the outset in an arresting paradox. "The Christian man is a perfectly free lord of all, subject to none" (*"omnium dominus est liberrimus, nulli subjectus"*). Yet "the Christian man is a perfectly dutiful servant of all, subject to all" (*"omnium servus est officiosissimus, omnibus subjectus"*).

These seemingly contradictory statements are based on certain phrases from St. Paul (I Corinthians 9:19; Romans 13:8) and upon the fact that Christ the Lord made himself servant of all. Externals such as priestly robes or ascetic works do not affect Christian righteousness or liberty. The soul can do without all things except the Word of God; having that, and nothing else, it is rich in all blessings. Christ came for the ministry of the Word, and for that the priesthood exists. This Word of God is the Gospel of God concerning his Son. Faith alone is the saving and efficacious use of the Word. (*Fides enim sola est salutaris et efficax usus verbi Dei*). The soul is justified by faith alone, and not by any works. The inner man cannot be justified and set free by any outward work: one must lay aside all trust in works. Faith is an incomparable treasure, bringing a complete salvation.

The Scripture contains commands and promises. The commands, such as "Thou shalt not covet," serve to humiliate us; by enforcing the lesson of our inability to satisfy the law, they condition us to accept the promises. The promises say to us: "Believe, and you shall have all," and they supply the fulfillment of the commands. The Christian is set free from the law by faith:

And this is Christian liberty, even our faith, which does not indeed cause us to live in idleness or in wickedness, but makes the law and works unnecessary for any man's righteousness or salvation.

Unnecessary for salvation but, be it noted, not in any sense unnecessary for the Christian life.

Faith, moreover, so trusts God as to honor Him, ascribing to Him all truthfulness and righteousness and wholly consenting to His will. This obedience of faith makes our own works (as an agency in salvation) superfluous: in them a man would be denying God and making an idol of himself. Faith, honoring God, is rewarded by His counting the soul righteous for faith's sake. So Abraham's faith "was counted unto him for righteousness" (Romans 4:3).

Thirdly, faith unites the soul with Christ as a spotless bride with her bridegroom. Here we have the theme of the mystical marriage, Christ the bridegroom of the devout soul —a theme enlarged upon by countless medieval mystics. Luther ties the thought with an evangelical concept of salvation. The gifts of Christ, His grace and sacrificial righteousness, redeem the soul and give it victory over sin and death. The commandment to worship one God can be fulfilled only by the faith that ascribes to Him all goodness and claims nothing for human works. Yet the works men do in faith may be done to God's glory.

United with Christ, the believer partakes of His spiritual kingship and priesthood. Christ imparts these to the soul, as the bridegroom shares with the bride what he possesses. Christians may suffer and die; but they share a power that is Christ's, a spiritual dominion. "I have need of nothing except that faith exercise the power and dominion of its own liberty." So the Christian is a king and lord of all things.

In Christ, moreover, we are not only kings but priests, which is "more excellent." Here Luther treats a favorite topic, the priesthood of all Christians. All believers share in the priesthood of Christ. This means that they pray for others and teach one another the things of God. Although we are equally priests yet we cannot all publicly minister and teach. Christ should be preached, not merely historically, and not so as to create sympathy for Him and anger against

Jews and such "childish nonsense," but so as to establish
faith, "that He may be Christ for thee and for me." Through
our faith His victory over death and sin becomes our victory.
We share, by faith alone, the glory of Christ's kingly and
priestly status. To seek salvation by works instead is like
the behavior of the dog in the fable that dropped the bone
to seek its reflected shadow.

IV

This exalted faith-mysticism of Luther may seem to be
morally indifferent, or even to lead to the negation of
morals. Some, he notes, may say: Very well then, we will
do no works and be content with faith. "Not so, ye wicked
men," answers Luther. So long as he lives in the flesh, the
Christian is servant of all and does all manner of works.
Luther uses two main categories of good works. The Christian must govern his body, and he must have right relations
with his fellow men. The inward man, triumphant in faith,
"with joyful zeal" strives to subject the body, to crucify
the flesh. Such efforts or works do not justify: but they
spontaneously arise from the faith that justifies. Adam in his
unfallen state, and needing no meritorius works, dressed and
kept the garden. Good works do not make a man good; a
good man does good works, just as the fruits do not bear
the tree but the tree the fruits, and as a good or bad house
does not make, but is made by, a good or a bad builder.
Nothing makes a man good except faith, or evil except unbelief. Our works only expose the good or evil in us. Luther's
position is: We cherish good works, but deny that they
have saving power. The teaching of repentence is vain without the teaching of faith.

For repentance proceeds from the law of God but faith or
grace from the promise of God . . . so that a man is consoled

and exalted by faith in the divine promise, after he has been humbled and led to a knowledge of himself by the threats and fear of the divine law.

The Christian, too, has obligations to his neighbor. He does not live for himself, but for all men on earth: indeed, he lives only for others (*immo solum aliis vivit et non sibi*). He disciplines his body that he may serve others, and he can never be idle in this service. The need and advantage of his neighbor should govern all his work. He trains himself to bear the burdens of others.

Lo, this is a truly Christian life, here faith is truly effectual through love: that is, it issues in works of the freest service cheerfully and lovingly done, with which a man willingly serves another without hope of reward [*qua alteri gratis et sponte servit*], and for himself is satisfied with the fulness and wealth of his faith.

Since each has abundant riches in his faith, his good works are a surplus that he can use to do good to his neighbor. This theme is expanded with quotations from Philippians and Galatians. As God has dealt with him, the Christian will deal with his neighbor. In happy realization of his God-given spiritual wealth, he freely and joyfully seeks to do all that is pleasing to a God so gracious. "I will therefore," says Luther boldly, "give myself as a Christ to my neighbor" (*"Dabo itaque me quendam Christum, proximo meo"*) doing nothing but what is profitable to him, and taking no account of gratitude or ingratitude, gain or loss. "We ought freely to help our neighbor through our body and its works . . . that we may be Christs to one another" (*"ut simus mutuum Christi"*).

Thus the paradox with which the book began comes to be resolved. The Christian sharing Christ's victory is lord over sin and death, and in gratitude for Christ's sacrifice gladly serves his fellow men. By numerous examples from the New Testament Luther distinguishes works done for merit from works done "freely and joyfully for the sake of others." Vain, he fears, are those works of colleges, monasteries, altars and offices of the Church in which "we seek our own profit," in ignorance of Christian liberty. Take heed, he warns, that your prayers, fasts and philanthropies are done not to gain some benefit, temporal or eternal, but only that others may profit from them.

V

This, then, is Christian freedom according to Luther. It springs from faith and rightly accompanies the good works that are the spontaneous expression of faith. It involves the priesthood of every Christian; each helps others Godward and yields service to others in life's common tasks. Faith, priesthood and freedom for Luther do not make us individualistic, isolated or negative toward spiritual and social fellowship. On the contrary he lays stress on the activity of fellowship and on the Christian's primary concern for other men.

See [he writes, in what was at first intended as the conclusion], according to this rule the good things we have from God should flow from one to the other and be common to all. . . . From Christ they have flowed and are flowing into us. . . . From us they flow on to those that have need of them. . . . A Christian man lives not in himself but in Christ and his neighbor. Otherwise he is not a Christian. He lives in Christ through faith, in his neighbor through love.

But now, to avoid being misunderstood, he decides to add a few afterthoughts. He vigorously disavows those who when Christian liberty is affirmed make it the occasion of fleshly license or of the mere despising of religious ceremonies. To refuse to fast and to scoff "with upturned nose" at the precepts of men—these do not make men free or

Christian. Equally in error are those who rest their salvation on the observance of ceremonies and precepts, caring not a fig for faith. "Our faith in Christ does not free us from works, but from false opinions concerning works." There is, perhaps, some lack of complete consistency here with what has gone before: but it is not a reversal of the main direction of the thought. The point of emphasis is, as before, that works do not save. His advice is that we ought to shock the stubborn ceremonialists by free breaking of the rules of fasting, but that in charity we ought to avoid offending the simple-minded, who cannot yet grasp the conception of liberty. Love demands this, for love would harm none and serve all. We must fight against the wolves, but for the sheep. We cannot live without ceremonies; but as honors test humility, and fasts, temperance, so ceremonies are the test of the righteousness of faith. Again, they are like the architect's models and plans; when the structure is completed they are laid aside. We do not despise ceremonies and works; we despise the false estimate of them. Nature and reason are weak and tend to overestimate laws and works. There is need that God himself should teach us, and make us *theodacti*,[3] taught of God. After referring to "godless and blind popes" he closes with a benediction upon his friends and foes.

VI

Luther's own evaluation of the booklet is given at the end of his letter to Leo: "It is a small thing if thou regard its bulk, but unless I am deceived, it is the whole of Christian living in brief form." He thought of it as a compendium, not of formal theology, but of the practical principles of the Christian life. It is not easy to equate it with the labored,

[3] Θεοδίδακτοι, as in I Thessalonians 4:9, "Ye yourselves are taught of God to love one another."

analytic statements of belief that are found in long theological treatises and in formal confessions of faith. Nevertheless it contains the simple elements of the experience and
practice of Christian living. Luther's commanding paradox
makes sense, I think, to the religious soul: free lord of all,
dutiful servant of all. On the one hand the truly religious
man has in his faith a secret exaltation, a mastery of circum-
stance, an emancipation from fear of men and events. He is
not to be cowed or bullied or dismayed. On the other hand,
in gratitude for this liberating experience, he devotes himself to self-discipline and acts of blessing to others, regarding himself as debtor to all and servant of all.

When Luther says he has set down here "the whole of
Christian living in brief form," he is taking a firm position
on the question of what is essential Christianity. He is extolling faith as the key to salvation. The theme runs through
all his major utterances. It is unforgettably expressed in a
few pages of his Preface to the *Epistle to the Romans*. I
quote (modernizing the spelling) from the English edition
of 1632 which I believe was the one Wesley heard at the
meeting in Aldersgate Street, May 24, 1738, when that later
reformer's heart was "strangely warmed."[4] The translation
is made from the Preface as expanded by Luther's close associate, Justus Jonas (1523).

But a true Faith is the work of God whereby we are regenerate and born anew by his Spirit. . . . Wherefore faith is such
an effectual, lively, quick and mighty operation in our heart,
that it cannot be idle, but must needs break out and shew itself
by good works. . . . Faith therefore is a constant trust and a
sure confidence of the mercy of God towards us, which is lively
and worketh mightily in our hearts, whereby we commit ourselves wholly to God, casting all our care upon him: leaning
and trusting assuredly in this faith we are not afraid to die a
thousand times.

[4] See below, chap. vi, note 5.

Luther believed that in such expressions he was rightly interpreting the thought of St. Paul in Romans. The whole drift of this epistle, he says, is that by faith alone we are justified, and that of necessity works follow faith: "Wheresoever faith is, it cannot choose but work: like as the flame cannot but give good light."

VII

This spontaneous, enthusiastic and energetic religion involves also the social implications suggested by the doctrine of the priesthood of believers. A further word on that topic may be in order. Luther argues elsewhere, from I Peter 2:9 and Revelation 5:10, that all Christians are in Scripture called priests. The special public liturgical exercise of this power is by special ordination. When a bishop consecrates he acts on behalf of all. If a little group of lay Christians were taken captive and isolated they could lawfully choose and charge one of their members to perform the public offices of the ministry. In permitting lay baptism under necessity the Church recognizes the lay priesthood. But for the very reason that all Christians are priests, no one may take on the public function without due consent and election. "For what is common to all, no one dare take upon himself without the will and consent of the community." In numerous passages Luther takes this position. The public priesthood or ministry is a necessity, but it is thought of as a representative office, not as the function of a spiritual caste whose members have an indelible character through ordination. For malfeasance, the officeholder is deposed and reduced, so to speak, to his private rank.[5] "Priests, as we call them, are ministers chosen from among us, who do all that they do in our

[5] *Address to the Nobility.*

name."[6] In his Advice to the Estates of Bohemia, 1523,[7] Luther again draws the contrast between the priesthood that is "spiritual and common" and that which is "special and external." The latter is not to be exercised "except by consent of the whole body or church" ("*nisi consensu universitatis seu ecclesiae*").

From these and similar passages it seems justifiable to say that they err greatly who suppose the logical outworking of Luther's principle of lay priesthood to be the elimination of any specialized ministry. Luther entertained no such possibility. He would have seen nothing to be gained and very much to be lost by it. His teaching on the ministry is low from the point of view of "order," but high from the point of view of qualifications. He guards the ministry with the greatest jealously, providing for the education and testing of candidates. The former ordinations of pastors were not called in question in the churches that became Lutheran; but when recruits were needed a new form of ordination was introduced (1525). In accordance with Luther's view, the Augsburg Confession states in its fourteenth article: "That no one should publicly teach in the church or administer the sacraments unless he is regularly called" ("*nisi rite vocatus*"). Lutherans have differed with regard to what is meant by "regularly called;" but they agree that some external form of admission to the office of a minister of the Word and sacraments is needful.

So much for the public exercise of the priestly function. In his private role the Christian does, however, constantly exercise his priesthood. We can all, as Luther says, "pray for one another;" we can, in fact, be "Christs one to an-

---

[6] *Babylonish Captivity:* "Ordination."

[7] *De Instituendis ministris Ecclesiae. Werke* (Weimar Ausgabe), XII, 180 ff. Cf. J. T. McNeill, *Unitive Protestantism* (New York: Abingdon Press, 1930), pp. 122 f.

other." As priests also, he tells us in the *Letter to the Nobility*, magistrates cobblers, smiths, farmers serve in their daily tasks, by many kinds of work contributing to "the bodily and spiritual welfare of the community." Mainly, and constantly, through his calling, the Christian serves all whom he touches. This vocational service is thought of as hallowed, and as belonging within the province of the good works prompted by faith. Dr. E. R. Kiessling, in a study of Luther's sermons of the period of our treatise, refers to Luther's "social gospel" in these words:

He points out that God requires only faith for Himself. Every other expression of the Christ spirit within us belongs to the neighbor. The Christian must go out of his way to find and help the poor, the sick, and the frail. He must learn to associate with the stubborn, the foolish, the proud and other unpleasant types of people. . . . A Christian lives in this world not to find, but to make, pious, righteous and holy people, just as he also seeks to make rich, strong, and healthy those who are poor, weak, and sick.[8]

VIII

It is in this frame of ideas then, that Luther proclaims the liberty of a Christian man. Clearly enough, he saw that this inner freedom was something that affected the whole social behavior of the Christian. So far as this treatise is concerned, it is left unrelated to any claim of political liberty. It involves liberty of conscience, but liberty of conscience is not thought of as a thing that the state can give or take away.

A series of writers subsequent to Luther have led us to appreciate the necessity of associating liberty of conscience with civil liberty. We recognize the fact that historically

[8] *The Early Sermons of Luther* (Grand Rapids: Zondervan, 1935), p. 106.

political liberty has grown largely from the assertion of claims of conscience against the state. Luther did not see the point that the liberty of a Christian man would in practice involve free and responsible citizenship. As a consequence of this, and of his reliance upon the princes in the authorization of reforms and the reordering of the Church, he has been charged with political absolution and reactionism. It is alleged that he was responsible for the inception of an era of ecclesiastical compliance toward the state, which in our own century has proved disastrous for Germany and for the world. In the midst of World War II, W. R. Inge wrote:

If we wish to find a scapegoat on whose shoulders we may lay the miseries which Germany has brought upon the world— not, perhaps, a very scientific way of writing history—I am more and more convinced that the worst evil genius of that country is not Hitler or Bismarck or Frederick the Great, but Martin Luther.

He quoted Troeltsch's affirmation that Luther's doctrine of obedience "glorifies power for its own sake; it therefore glorifies whatever authority may happen to be dominant at any given time." This Dr. Inge thinks very much like the notorious doctrine of Machiavelli, and like that of Hobbes.[9] This is an extreme statement of a position taken by numerous critics of Luther in the past century. It has frequently been answered and as frequently revived. Since Dr. Inge's declaration, Peter F. Wiener has presented a pamphlet entitled *Martin Luther, Hitler's Spiritual Ancestor*, to which Gordon Rupp has replied in *Martin Luther, Hitler's Cause— or Cure*.[10] Mr. Rupp has brought a weight of evidence to show that large elements in Luther have to be omitted in this Luther-to-Hitler theory and that specific misrepresen-

[9] *The Churchman*, October 15, 1944.
[10] Both books appeared in London in 1945.

tations are utilized to support it; and he concludes that "the line runs straight from Luther away from Hitler."

It is unfortunate that the evaluation of Luther should be rendered difficult for us by emotions generated in ecclesiastical antipathies and the sufferings of war; but it is a condition that we ought to recognize and to be able to reckon with. Dr. Inge at least acknowledges the fact that the quest of some scapegoat among historical personalities is "not a very scientific way of writing history." As one who has given a good deal of attention to the reformer's political thought, I feel justified in saying that Luther would have abhorred Hitler and all his works. He would probably have condemned him as he did Sickingen and the Knights in 1522, or aroused the weak politicians to action against him in the way in which he called the princes to suppress the Peasant Revolt in 1525.

Yet it is fair to admit that Luther had an exaggerated respect for the "powers ordained of God" and to recognize as in part a result of this the prevailing submissiveness toward the state which marks the history of German Lutheranism. The fact that in the Scandinavian lands the Lutheran witness against tyranny has often been vigorous ought to make us free to discount such generalizations as that of Dr. Inge. The whole question of the relation of Luther to historic Lutheranism cannot be answered simply, and this is especially true of matters of political and social ethics.[11] Luther was not ready to espouse political democracy as the natural concomitant of the liberty of faith. It is always pos-

[11] Carl Meyer in "The Crisis of German Protestantism," *Social Research*, XII (1945), 397-442, presents an acute analysis of the social attitudes of modern German Lutheranism and of the influences playing upon it in recent times. Cf. A. L. Drummond, "Church and State in Protestant Germany, with Special References to Prussia," *Church History*, XIII (1944), 210-229.

sible for his readers to take that step. But the essential purpose of the book is a purely religious one. We may reflect that although the outward guarantees of political liberty are commonly assumed to be valuable and precious to those who have them, they are undefended and soon surrendered by men who cease to prize the inner deliverance and to stand fast in the liberty of their souls. There is no substitute for the freedom that is within the breast. This freedom Luther found and extolled. He proclaimed deliverance through faith from the oppression of works of merit that are never completed, and a resulting happy activity in works of service to men.

Luther has been under constant attack ever since his battle began. By many of his utterances he has invited attack. To this particular book, however, his critics have given very slight attention. Thoughtful men of religion will always differ on the validity, and the value, of the exclusive claims Luther made for his own type of religious experience. The Canons of the Council of Trent anathematize those who affirm justification by faith alone. Yet neither does Luther teach that good works are needless nor do Roman Catholics teach that faith is needless. They hold that works secure future merit and have a saving value, while Luther holds that works are not meritorious or a cause of salvation, but a consequence of the faith in which salvation lies. The difference will not soon be resolved. Whatever our own convictions, we shall do well to hold them with greater charity than was shown by the disputants of the sixteenth century. In these perplexing and soul-shattering times many at least feel as Luther did the untrustworthiness of human works and motives and the inescapable necessity of a venture of faith by which all the insecurity of reliance upon our faulty moral effort is transcended. In that experience, moral action begins anew under the impulse of faith. It would seem that a consideration of this utterance of sincere conviction and piety, put forth amid the controversies of a fighting reformer, might prove a source of spiritual invigoration to many, from whatever angle of approach they come to its vivid pages.

JOHN CALVIN:

Institutes of the Christian Religion

Chapter II

JOHN CALVIN:

Institutes of the Christian Religion

At the end of August, 1535, when Calvin gave Thomas Platter, the Basel printer, the manuscript of his *Institutio religionis Christianae*, he had just entered his twenty-seventh year. The young theologian had been well schooled from childhood, and his studies had embraced most aspects of the learning of his time. As an undergraduate of the University of Paris he had undoubtedly been aware of the conflict of the new scholarship of the French Renaissance with the traditional education and theology. During his law studies at Orléans and Bourges, his interest in humanism had increased. In both these centers he had enjoyed the instruction not only of eminent jurists but also of the German humanist Melchior Wolmar, with whom he began the study of Greek. Wolmar was favorable to Lutheranism, but it does not appear that he disturbed Calvin's early religious conservatism. Calvin was on the conservative side also in a dispute in legal circles. The position of his admired law master, Pierre de l'Étoile, was challenged by the brilliant Renaissance legal scholar, Andrea Alciati of Milan, whom Francis I had invited to Bourges. One of Calvin's numerous scholarly friends, Nicholas Duchemin, published in 1531 a controversial tract favorable to L'Étoile, and for this Calvin wrote a prefatory letter—the first fragment from his pen to appear in print.[1]

When Calvin's father, who had induced him to study law, died in May, 1531, the youth turned to the more congenial field of classical literature. He took up residence again in Paris, and became a pupil of the Royal Lecturers then recently appointed by the king to give instruction in Latin, Greek and Hebrew, and especially of Pierre Danès, who taught Greek. Danès had come under the influence of Jacques Lefèvre, whose work on the Scriptures marks a transition from medieval to Reformation concepts. There is no adequate evidence that Calvin had yet any thought of moving into a Protestant position. He tried out his now well-formed Latin style not in a Bible commentary but in his distinctly humanistic *Commentary on Seneca's Treatise on Clemency* (1532). This book, loaded with classical allusions, and with remarkably few citations of Scripture, shows a critical appropriation of Stoicism where that philosophy stresses conscience and humane government. It was a serious, if somewhat pedantic, book; but it made no perceptible impression, and its author may have felt the relative futility of the humanistic approach to the insistent problems of an age increasingly involved in religious conflict.

Another of his humanist friends was Nicholas Cop, who belonged to a family distinguished for learning and who was now chosen rector of the university. Cop's rectorial address, November 1, 1533, was a bold challenge to the old theology of the Sorbonne doctors, without any suggestion, however, of rejection of the authority of the papal church. Calvin was associated with the authorship of the address, and to escape persecution made his escape from Paris. Some would have us believe that Calvin was at that time a convinced Protes-

[1] On these matters see especially Q. Breen, *John Calvin: a Study in French Humanism* (Grand Rapids: Eerdmans, 1931), chaps. i–iv.

tant. It seems more in accord with the known facts to suppose that he was now engaged in an inward struggle that led to what he calls in 1559 his "sudden conversion," and that this experience is to be dated half a year later than Cop's address. Though Calvin speaks of his conversion as "sudden," he represents it as a delayed surrender to the will of God. In the following April he visited the now very aged Lefèvre, who, proscribed in France, had found protection in Nérac. It may even have been his interview with this revered teacher—whose dynamic ideas in theology had been rendered ineffectual through his ecclesiastical caution—that brought the young scholar to the point of decision. At any rate he promptly gave evidence of a new resolution. He went to Noyon, his birthplace, and resigned the church incomes that had been secured for him there in his childhood (May 4, 1534).

II

Two writings of Calvin as a Protestant preceded the *Institutes*. One of these was called *Psychopannychia*, which, as its title implies, dealt with the question of the "sleep of the soul" between death and the resurrection. Against Anabaptist opinions, Calvin denied that the soul is unconscious in this interval. Calvin may have realized that he was here dealing with theologically peripheral matters, for the treatise, written in 1534, remained unpublished for eight years.

His full enlistment in the cause of the Reformation is indicated in two prefaces which he wrote for the French translation of the Bible, prepared by his cousin Pierre Robert Olivétan for the Waldenses of Piedmont and published early in 1535. One is a preface to the Bible as a whole, the other to the New Testament. In the latter he writes as one of the persecuted evangelicals whom he exhorts to be steadfast: "If we are banished from one country, the earth is the Lord's. If we are cast out of the earth, we are not thereby cast out of God's Kingdom."

Theodore Beza, who wrote a Life of Calvin shortly after the latter's death, states that the *Institutes* was written in 1534. The date is probably a year too early. In the preface to his *Commentary on the Psalms* Calvin indicates the circumstances, and his reasons for writing the book. He had gone to Basel, and there had been aware that in France many people were being burned for their faith. Lying pamphlets were being circulated to the effect that the victims were Anabaptists and seditious persons only. He felt that it would be cowardice or treachery not to come to the defense of his persecuted fellow believers. His hope was, by expounding their beliefs, "to vindicate my brethren whose death was precious in the sight of the Lord" and "that foreign nations might be touched with at least some compassion toward them."

This situation accords with the facts of 1535. At the beginning of that year Calvin was in Basel. Serious persecution had begun the previous October; in the early months of 1535 it became severe. Melanchthon wrote of it as "savage cruelty against wise and pious men." The French king, on February 1, sent a letter to the German princes of the Schmalkald League (the Lutheran alliance) stating that those punished were political traitors. Francis I, indeed, entertained plans of Church reform. He had clerical agents observing events in Germany, and on June 23, 1535, invited Melanchthon to assist in framing an ecclesiastical constitution for France. It was plain, however, that he would not permit such a reordering of religion as would satisfy Protestants. Melanchthon finally declined the royal invitation on August 28. In August Calvin had finished writing the *Institutes*. He then penned a brilliant plea on behalf of his coreligionists, addressed to the French king, which was to serve as introduction to the book.

This introductory address "to His Most Christian Majesty Francis, King of the French" suggests, indeed, that the work had been begun as a modest exposition of the evangelical faith for the use of inquirers "hungering and thirsting after Christ," but that the plan had been somewhat altered as a result of the increase of persecution, so as to make it not merely a summary of doctrine but a defense of Protestantism. Francis is here solemnly warned against the false accusations that are spread abroad and the iniquitous decisions of judges who turn their prejudices into sentences. Where all others in authority are misled, let the king maintain the glory of God and rule by His Word. Calvin excoriates the priests who, having neither knowledge nor piety, in order to secure their own fat livings incite the persecutors and falsely charge the evangelicals with embracing a new Gospel contrary to the teaching of the Church Fathers. By many references to the Fathers, he claims their sanction for his scriptural faith. He attacks the assumption that the reforming party are hostile to the Church. The Church is perpetually sustained by Christ, even though her outward form may not always be apparent. She exists not in external splendor, but wherever the Word is truly preached and the sacraments rightly administered, even though outwardly she is oppressed and obscured, as in the days of Elijah. Those who uphold the papal church are compared with the four hundred false prophets of Ahab's time and with the very respectable Sanhedrin that sought the death of Christ. Some disturbances have indeed arisen, but only because Satan is always aroused against the Word of God. Calvin haughtily denies the politically and morally subversive purpose with which he and his friends are charged. He writes in the hope of overcoming the king's known antipathy: if this fails and imprisonments, tortures and burnings continue, the afflicted will possess their souls in patience, awaiting divine deliverance and vindication.

There is no evidence that Francis ever saw the volume which contained these vigorous pages. Before its publication, in the following March, Calvin had departed to Ferrara.

It has often been remarked, and it is substantially true, that Calvin never altered his teachings after the appearance of the first edition of the *Institutes*. "In the doctrine which he taught in the beginning," says Beza, "he remained firm to the end." But the alterations made in later editions were not merely expansions. The work was consciously transformed. At first an apologetic for the French Protestants, it was turned into a systematic treatise "to train candidates in sound theology." This is the aim of the second edition, published at Strasbourg in 1539. Like the first it was in Latin. At least ten, perhaps twelve, Latin editions appeared in Calvin's lifetime, culminating in the basic revision of 1559. The French edition of 1541 was the author's own translation of the second Latin edition, and was the only French translation that was certainly made by Calvin himself. A French version apparently not by Calvin was made in 1560 from the 1559 Latin text, and was seven times reprinted before Calvin died.

In his preface to the final Latin edition Calvin indicates that he has been stimulated by the wide demand for the work repeatedly to enlarge and improve it. He further states that he has always felt dissatisfied with it until it could be reconstructed in the form now presented. When during the previous winter a quartan fever had led him to expect death, he had redoubled his efforts to complete it, as a legacy to the religious public and a service to the Church of God. The revision involved an extensive reshaping, and a substantial enlargement, of the treatise. It was now, in fact, five times the size of the first edition. It was divided into four books so arranged as to offer a systematic treatment of the whole body of Christian theology. The titles of the four books follow the topics of the Apostles' Creed—the Father, the Son, the Holy Spirit and the Holy Catholic Church.

III

In the first book of the *Institutes* Calvin is concerned with the knowledge of God as Creator. He affirms at the outset that our true wisdom consists in the knowledge of God and of ourselves, and we cannot know either without some knowledge of the other. Thus if we examine ourselves we become aware that the gifts with which we are endowed come not from ourselves but from God, in whom we live and move and have our being. Our very defects lead us to the same dependence on God: our ignorance, misery and depravity remind us by contrast of the infinite riches of his wisdom, goodness, purity and justice. Nor can we truly understand ourselves until we have learned by contemplating the divine perfections how worthless is our pretense of virtue. Accordingly in the Scripture saintly men who find themselves in the presence of God are overwhelmed with dread of His majesty and convinced of their own unworthiness.

God is manifest to men in general as Creator; He appears in Christ as Redeemer. While Scripture presents both of these manifestations of the divine nature, it is the former that is the topic here. Calvin at once takes his ground in religion rather than in philosophy. He dismisses the thought of a speculative inquiry divorced from piety, and he defines piety as "reverence joined with love of God, which a knowledge of his benefits induces." He refuses to search out what (*quid*) God is, but asks rather what kind of being (*qualis*)

He is in His relationship with man and nature.[2] No Epicurean deity, indifferent, indolent and inaccessible, would be worth serious thought. The idea of God should be accompanied by grateful obedience to His will as "the law of our lives." Nor, says Calvin, can your idea of God be clarified unless you acknowledge Him the fount and origin of every good (I, ii, 2).

Thus we are led to anticipate a strictly theological and directly constructive discussion. Calvin will rest his argument upon the ground of Scripture: but he is far from contending that man has no knowledge of God apart from Scripture. Some awareness of the existence of God has been implanted in the human mind, and this is shared even by the dullest and most degraded races of men. The universality of religion is evidence that some sense of divinity is inscribed in the hearts of all men. Even idolatry testifies to this fact. That religion arises from the crafty devices of those who seek control over their fellows is an absurd view. Even persons who affirm their atheism are haunted with fear of the divine. Others, wishing to avoid obedience to God, tremble amid their resistance and evasion, or hypocritically yield a worship of trivial sacrifices and observances. All such wayward behavior in religion is taken as supporting the thesis that even bad men retain a sense of God that has been naturally engraved on their hearts.

The long fifth chapter of Book I sets forth in eloquent and moving phrases the glory of God as revealed in the beauty and order of the universe, which is such that men cannot open their eyes without beholding Him. "Wherever you cast your eye," says Calvin, "there is no particle of the world in which some sparks at least of His glory cannot be observed to shine," while the whole fair structure overwhelms us with an immensity of splendor (*vi immensa ful-*

[2] Cf. I, x, 2: "*Non quis sit apud se, sed qualis erga nos.*"

goris). The proofs of God's wisdom are not only shown to the experts in astronomy, medicine or the natural sciences but thrust before the illiterate peasant. They appear in the orderly array of the unnumbered stars and in the symmetry and beauty of the human frame. Man is rightly called a microcosm, for he contains within himself the marvels of creation, and it is inexcusable on our part that we are too slothful to "descend within ourselves" that we may find God. Alas, that men should fail to extol God for their talents, but instead make these the occasion of vainglory; that they should even use their God-given faculties to argue that God is not, or that nature, which God has made and ordered, is itself God. The study of the divine power and perfections, as manifested in earth and sky, is open to those without, as well as those within, the circle of His favor. The observation of natural events leads us to recognize that God is the self-existent and eternal source of all things, and that His creation and preservation of the world have no cause other than His goodness, which is more than sufficient to deserve the response of our love.

The theme here changes to the special providences that appear in human affairs such as deliverances of the distressed, captives, the shipwrecked and the sick; raising the lowly; casting down the proud. Providence, and not chance, rules this realm, though only one in a hundred seeing the evidence really sees God's glory in it. The afflictions of the pious and the injustices which God now leaves unpunished are intimations of a future life in which these inequalities will be corrected.

Thus all God's works mirror His divine perfections. Rightly to contemplate these, we must "descend into ourselves" and consider how He exercises in and toward us His wisdom, power, righteousness, goodness and mercy. But actually we are blind and inattentive to the facts of creation and providence. The philosophers, even Plato with his globe (in *Timaeus*), fail us here. They have darkened the question with disputations. Nations and individuals have adopted base notions of deity or in perplexity turned to the worship of an unknown God. God graciously allures men to a knowledge of Himself, but they wilfully pursue paths of error. The bright lamps lighted in the universe to show God's glory shine in vain. The dullness of our mind is caused by sin, and we are inexcusable—convicted by our own consciences of sloth and ingratitude.

For the salvation of man thus incapacitated by sin, there arises the necessity of the Scripture revelation. Scripture is like the lenses that enable those of dull vision to read. In it God speaks of Himself both as Creator and as Redeemer and of the worship due to Him. The authority of Scripture does not rest upon the declaration of the Church, but in the conviction that God is its author. Our guide to the understanding of Scripture is "the inward testimony of the Spirit," which is superior to reason and argumentation. Scripture thus speaks to the believer who is eager to hear God's Word: others miss its message and remain ignorant of God. Yet Calvin produces a long array of rational arguments for the divine authorship of the Bible, amid which we read that "the consent of the Church is not without weight," since it arose from an acceptance of the canonical books in all parts of the early Church (I, viii, 11). Calvin's emphasis on the testimony of the Spirit is vigorously guarded against the doctrine of the Libertines or "Spirituals" who assumed the sufficiency of their own inspirations without attention to the Word.

What, then, do the Scriptures teach concerning God? They corroborate the evidence of His works, as is illustrated by a single Psalm (the 145th), a summary of all divine perfections, which yet contains nothing but what may be observed in created things. Three attributes of God are given high importance: mercy, judgment and righteousness. These presuppose that He also possesses truth, power, goodness and holiness. The knowledge of God afforded by Scripture does not differ from that which we might learn from the works of creation, and is similarly designed to lead us to true worship. It calls men back to belief in one God, a principle known but inexcusably forsaken by idolatrous men.

An extended denunciation of idolatry is here introduced (I, xi; xii). All material representation of deity is condemned. The Hebrew cherubim are thought of as belonging to a stage of puerility that has now been passed. Calvin challenges Gregory the Great's approval of pictures, and quotes the decision of the Synod of Elvira (305) against their use. Sculpture and painting he acknowledges to be gifts of God; but they are not to be used to represent things invisible. The distinction of *latria* and *dulia* (worship and service), employed to excuse the honoring of images, affords no justification of the practice, in which the glory of God is diminished.

The treatment of the doctrine of the Trinity (I, xii)—a section greatly expanded in the final edition of the work—is replete with citations from the Fathers. Calvin (like many a modern student) would be glad, if it were possible, to abandon the terms employed in the Arian controversy, since they were not consistently used or correctly translated from Greek into Latin. Why should *homoousios* become in Latin *consubstantialis*, confusing "essence" and "substance"? He would be satisfied with so brief a declaration as: "that the Father, the Son and the Spirit are one God; and yet neither is the Son the Father nor the Spirit the Son, but they are distinct by a certain property." However, the orthodox Fathers have Calvin's sympathy as they labored with terms to save the faith. In John 1:1 he finds the divine *essence* ("was God") and the *subsistence* of the Person ("was with God") affirmed of Christ. He makes liberal use of Old Testament passages to support the deity both of Christ and of the Holy Spirit. Modern antitrinitarians, Servetus included, who seek to rekindle the embers of old controversy, are refuted at some length. Their appropriation of certain statements of Irenaeus incites Calvin to rescue "that holy man" from their company. Tertullian's conception of an "economy" in the Trinity is also explained in an orthodox sense. The tendency of Calvin's argument is to assert the equality of the Persons of the Trinity more explicitly than the Fathers had done—a tendency even more marked in his various controversial writings on the topic.[3]

The doctrine of God as Creator involves for Calvin a doctrine of man, the masterpiece of creation. He pauses to discuss the angels, which, though not referred to in the chapters on the creation in Genesis, are attested in Scripture as blessed spirits employed to minister to men, but not to be appealed to as intercessors between us and God. The devils, too, have a place in the account of creation: created as angels, they revolted and became the instruments of perdition to others. The hostile army of devils is "represented" in Scripture as having one prince, Satan. We are warned of the machinations of the devils; but Satan can really do nothing which God does not permit. We ought to view with pious delight the fair theater of the universe and to set deep in our hearts the greatness, wisdom and goodness of the divine Artificer. who shaped and ordered the heavens in their matchless beauty, setting the courses of the countless stars that in their movements measure the seasons and the days. The world is a "splendid mansion" prepared for man in creation,

[3] Cf. B. B. Warfield, *Calvin and Calvinism* (New York: Oxford University Press, 1931), chap. iv.

and all things were created "for the sake of man" (I, xiv, 20–22).

Man has been given not only a body but an immortal soul, and endowed with marvelous powers of intellect by which he can survey the universe and the ages of history, and form conceptions of God and ideas of virtue. These are the tokens of the fact that man is made in the image of God. This is what differentiates him from the lower species. But, alas, this image was almost destroyed through the fall of Adam. Hence man is subject to passion, ignorance, inconstancy, lack of skill, temptation. Of the original noble endowments of the soul—reason, a lamp to guide his way, and the power to choose in the light of reason—only ruins remain, save insofar as they are restored in the regenerate. The philosophers who emphasize reason and free choice overlook the fact that man has lost his original status.

Three chapters (I, xvi–xviii) are devoted to the providence of God in the government of the world and in the changes of individual lives. Calvin is anxious to combat the notion that anything happens by chance. It is the sovereign God who is the cause of all events, though He may employ the plans of men. He overrules all for good, even the activities of Satan. He arouses men to repentance and good actions; He does not repent of His own actions or annul His own decrees. Calvin stresses the value of belief in Providence as a basis of trust, resignation to God's will, freedom from fear in adversity and danger, and diligence in the duties of our calling. How God makes use of evil agents without being the author of sin is a theme expounded at length with scriptural examples and with appropriate quotations from Augustine. God hardened Pharaoh's heart (Exodus 4:21); and the death of Christ, wickedly planned by men, was predetermined by God (Acts 4:28). But God is not to be charged with the perfidy of Judas, nor Judas credited with the redemption of Christ's death (I, xviii, 4). Calvin feels the difficulty of this teaching, which he nevertheless finds inescapable in the light of Scripture. A more modern view of Scripture would have helped him here. But it would not resolve the enduring problem of the sovereignty of a good God and the evil of history. Calvin will yield nothing either of God's sovereign government or of His moral perfection; nor does he minimize the evil of the world. He can only urge the submissive acceptance of "what is clearly attested in Scripture," since to do otherwise is to cavil against God.

Thus he brings Book I to a close. In its later sections we find ourselves morally aggrieved and mentally exasperated. Surely, we say, we cannot rest with this. Men have striven, before and since Calvin, to resolve the good-God-and-bad-world paradox. Calvin confronts it, not as a problem for philosophy, but as a mystery for faith. But the lasting impression of the book as a whole is that of bold and reasoned affirmation. It affirms in sincere and masterly eloquence the God of the Bible, a God of majesty and power, of wisdom and goodness, of judgment and mercy, Maker and Ruler of the world.

IV

Book II has for its theme Christ's work of redemption. Man's desperate need of divine salvation fills the background of the stage. In our fallen nature we are blind to our own condition, and helpless to recover what Adam lost. Without divine grace we are totally possessed by sin. The Fathers have gone too far with the philosophers in admitting man's moral freedom; but Augustine is right in calling the will a slave and in stressing, in company with Chrysostom, the basic importance of humility. Even here Calvin recognizes, however, that something is left amid the ruin. What is left is valueless for salvation, but valuable for this mundane life. Some sparks still glow in man's nature which distinguish him from the brutes. As the latter are distinct from inanimate things by their possession of sense, man is their superior by the possession of reason. Man is by nature a social animal, instinctively inclined to prize an ordered life, as we see in the consent of nations to be ruled by laws. The human capacity to learn and ingenuity to invent are gifts of nature. The light of truth shines in the writings of heathen men.

If we hold that the Spirit of God is the one fountain of truth, we shall neither reject nor despise the truth itself, wherever it appears, unless we wish to be contemptuous of the Spirit of God.

The insights, virtues and services to society of profane and unbelieving men are gifts of God and not to be rejected. Calvin is here acknowledging what he sometimes calls *gratia generalis,* common grace. Grace and nature here seem to be drawn together, and Calvin sometimes thinks of common grace as a remainder of the primal endowment of nature. God is, in any case, its Author, though it operates in an area distinct from the realm of salvation. It is closely related to Calvin's doctrine of natural law which underlies his political theory.[4] Calvin holds with the whole theological tradition that the Ten Commandments constitute a summary of the natural moral law engraved on all men's hearts:

Moreover, that interior law which . . . is written and, as it were, stamped upon every heart dictates to us [*nobis dictat lex illa interior* . . .] the very things that are to be learned in the Two Tables (II, viii, 1).

Yet, through his dullness and neglect, man has not learned by natural law to serve God aright, and needs the written

[4] See my article, "Natural Law in the Thought of the Reformers," *Journal of Religion,* XXV (1946), 168–182, and the treatises there cited.

reaffirmation of it in the Commandments. Calvin here includes a vigorous exposition of each of the Commandments. Let us merely note some typical interpretations. From "showing mercy unto thousands" in the Second Commandment he argues the greatness of God's mercy. The "thousands" are thousands of generations, as against "the third and fourth generation" punished for the iniquity of their fathers. On the Fourth Commandment he indicates that the Jewish Sabbath is abrogated in Christianity. Though we rightly keep the Lord's day for worship and the remission of the labor of servants, it is not to be observed with the "scrupulous rigor" of Judaism, but for the good of the Church. Theft in the Eighth Commandment is made to include imposture, fraud and legal oppression to obtain another's property.

Calvin has passed the middle of Book II when he comes to deal explicitly with the doctrine of redemption in Christ. In the discussion of the Trinity in Book I, as we have seen, the deity of Christ has already been amply treated. Here he examines the relation of the Law and the Gospel. The Gospel does not abolish the Law but confirms the promises of the Old Testament. It was heralded by John the Baptist, who stands between the two dispensations. The full day was ushered in when Christ ascended to heaven. Two chapters (II, x, xi) are here inserted to show first the similarity and secondly the difference of the two Testaments of Scripture. Calvin finds anticipations of the Gospel in the Covenant of the Old Testament, which proceeded solely from the mercy of God. A growing anticipation of Christ is seen from the "feeble sparks" of the promise to Adam through the "enlarging light" of later revelation, until Christ, the Sun of Righteousness, illumined the world (II, x, 20). The New Testament advances from the inferior and veiled instruction of the Old to the full declaration of saving truth. In Judaism the Church was "in a state of childhood": the Jews were "led to Christ by the tuition of the Law" (Galatians 3:24). In the New Testament we pass from the literal to the spiritual, from the revelation of death and condemnation to deliverance and the favor of God, from image to reality, from bondage to liberty, and from national limitation to "the vocation of the Gentiles." What Calvin calls the "superiority" of the New Testament to the Old is exemplified by the fact that there are in the *Institutes* 3098 quotations from the former, 1755 from the latter.[5]

Resuming his treatment of the work of Christ, Calvin discusses his office as Mediator. Christ is truly man as well as truly God, and this was necessary that he might overcome the alienation of man from God. His obedience as a man was required in order to undo the disobedience of Adam. Ever on guard against a speculative theology, Calvin vigorously condemns the "frivolous" suggestion of Osiander, the Nuremberg theologian, that even if Adam had not sinned the Mediator would have been needed. In a chapter on the two natures in Christ (II, xiv) he follows firmly the pattern of Chalcedonian orthodoxy, rejecting alike "confusion" and "separation." He then proceeds to examine the three offices of Christ as Prophet, King and Priest. As Prophet, He is "anointed to preach good tidings" and (e.g., in the words, "Hear ye Him") holds authority beyond other teachers. Revealing a perfection of teaching, He has rendered additional prophecies superfluous. As King, He governs and defends His Church, and guarantees its permanency. It is for our benefit, not for His own, that He reigns in His spiritual kingdom, bestowing on us spiritual power and wealth that we may contend fearlessly against the devil, sin and death, and requiring our obedience. As Priest He offers Himself as a

[5] H. Clavier, *Études sur le Calvinisme* (Paris: Fischbacker, 1936), p. 87.

sacrifice to take away our sins, and becomes our intercessor, securing our reconciliation to God.

Calvin pursues his examination of the work of Christ as Redeemer in a consideration of His death, resurrection and ascension (II, xvi). By His death He liberated us from sin and death; by His resurrection He restored us to life and righteousness. Our sins are mortified in the communion of His cross, and through His resurrection we walk in newness of life. In His elevation to heaven He began His reign, extending His energizing power through heaven and earth, and opened up the way to the Kingdom of Heaven which had been closed by Adam's sin. The last chapter of the book (II, xvii) is designed to explain how Christ merited our salvation. The merit of Christ is to be associated with, and not set over against, the mercy of God; and the point is emphasized, against certain of the scholastics, that the merits He obtained were in no sense for Himself, who needed none, but for those whom He redeemed.

V

The work of the Holy Spirit in the souls of the elect is the subject of Book III. The Spirit is spoken of under the figures of water, since he refreshes and cleanses, and of fire, since he burns away our vices and inflames our hearts with love of God. Faith, the principal work of the Spirit, is more than assent to the Gospel history. It is "a firm and sure knowledge of the divine good will toward us, which, founded on the truth of the gratuitous promise of Christ, is sealed in our hearts by the Holy Spirit." When we consider the mercy of God available to ourselves, and not to others only, we obtain the confidence of faith and a serene conscience. The believer is assured that God is to him a benevolent Father. Faith in God's mercy toward us, once experienced is never lost.

Some of the elect, it is true, through defects of their faith, pass through times of deep anxiety; but Calvin denies that they ever cease to persevere. He thinks of the Christian as normally advancing from little faith to greater, as he arms himself from the Word of God. There is an element of mysticism here. We are to regard Christ as not without but within us, being united with us in a communion that daily becomes closer—a view supported by an extended quotation from St. Bernard. Faith begins in God's promise of salvation and can have no stability unless it relies on the mercy of God. The Holy Spirit illuminates the Word, and gradually increases the faith of the believer, and of the Church as it advances to perfection.

The Spirit also arouses in us repentance (*poenitentia*). Calvin here explains that he is deliberately postponing the topic of reconciliation, or justification by faith. But repentance also follows upon faith. It is defined as "the true conversion of our life to God." It is induced by fear of God, and consists in the mortification of the flesh and the vivification of the Spirit. The transformation is not merely in externals, but within the soul. It bears fruit in piety toward God, charity toward men and sanctification of life. Indeed, repentance is to be practiced throughout life. Calvin encourages a voluntary consultation of their pastors by those in distress for their sins. He would abolish the obligatory confession introduced in the Middle Ages, with the system of satisfactions; and he denounces from Scripture and history the attendant doctrines of purgatory and indulgences.

Here follows a penetrating treatment of Christian holiness and duty, the "rule" derived from Scripture for the "reformation" of the personal life. Not to live a dedicated life would be ingratitude for grace bestowed. We commit ourselves to the perfection of the Gospel, unattainable as it is in this life, ever pressing forward in holiness and right-

eousness and abandoning all selfish aims. Central in sanctification for Calvin is self-denial, which arises when we turn
our whole mind toward God. This Godward direction of
life induces humility and consideration for others. Calvin
urgently teaches that God's gifts to us are deposits held in
trust for our neighbor. Indeed our service is to be extended
to all who are in need of it. Thus self-denial is transmuted
into social helpfulness. If we reflect that all possess in some
measure the image of God, this should induce us "to embrace
them in the arms of our love." Our works of charity are not
rewarded by temporal success. The pious Christian must
banish the thought of worldly prosperity. Selfishly and
without God's blessing we may acquire vast wealth, but in
the end it will bring us to misery. The Christian will not
envy those who enrich themselves by evil means, though his
own affairs are unprosperous, nor become despondent when
afflicted by war or frost or hail or disease, or the cross of
persecution; he will patiently trust in God and render thanks
to Him for the salutary use of these tribulations. The Christian, who trusts himself to God's providence and care, dif-
fers from the philosopher, who resigns himself to necessity.
Meditation on the life to come, when we shall know the supreme felicity which is the fully realized presence of God,
elevates the soul above the delights and calamities of the
world.

Such is Calvin's treatment of what theology has tech-
nically called "sanctification" (III, i–ix). He goes on to
define the Christian's proper use of the good things of this
life. We are on pilgrimage to the celestial kingdom, and God
has created many things not only for our use but for our
delight as we journey. This is seen even in food and cloth-
ing, and in all graceful forms and pleasing odors. It is not
unpleasing to God to use his gifts of wine and oil, to enjoy
the color and the smell of flowers, to admire the beauty of

gold, silver, ivory and marble, things evidently made rather for delight than for utility. But all undue, or intemperate, or unthankful enjoyment of such things is earnestly condemned. All the gifts of God are entrusted to us and we must answer for our stewardship. Every man's calling is a post of service, and the lowliest may be important in God's sight.

Coming now to the postponed topic of justification, Calvin substantially follows Luther. God justifies the sinner who by faith lays hold on the righteousness of Christ by imputing to him that righteousness, so that while still a sinner he is regarded as righteous. Justification is thus God's acceptance of us "as if we were righteous," and forgiving our sins. It does not mean, as Osiander would have it, that God first makes us essentially righteous, but that he gratuitously regards us as such. Faith is its "instrumental cause," while the "efficient cause" is God's love. It is thus a gift of God's free grace by which our sins are remitted. It does not wait for our sanctification. Works and merit have nothing to do with it. Calvin repeats Luther's phrase "by faith alone" ("*sola fide*") (III, xi, 2, 19; xiv, 14, 21). Only when faith and the grace of God are already present are a man's works acceptable to God (III, xiv, 8, 17, 21). The contrary views of the Roman theologians are combated at some length.

A chapter on Christian liberty (III, xix) stresses the Christian's relation to God as child to Father, and warns against an unhealthy scrupulosity, such as would avoid laughter, or good food and wine, or music, or the possession of any property. Moderation, charity and a chaste mind are to be preserved, but we ought to use such liberty as conduces to the edification of our neighbor. Calvin follows this by a notable discourse on prayer, a topic which, like that of liberty, formed one of the six chapters of the first edition of the *Institutes*. Prayer is regarded as the principal exercise of faith, and a familiar intercourse between God and the soul. It is to be practiced with complete attentiveness, with a sincere feeling of our need, in humility and with assured hope. Public worship should express the glory of God; and singing, in a speech understood by the worshipers, is a great aid to the ardor of devotion. The petitions of the Lord's Prayer are interpreted, and it is regarded as our authoritative directory for prayer.

At this point (III, xxi) Calvin introduces the doctrine of election or predestination. This is his definition:

> Predestination we call the eternal decree of God by which he has determined with himself what he would have to become of every man. For they are not all created in an equal condition; but eternal life is foreordained for some and eternal damnation for others. Every man therefore, being formed for one or the other of these ends, we say that he is predestinated to life or to death (III, xxi, 5).

The elect are wholly undeserving; the cause of their election is not in them but in God. Calvin favors Augustine and Bernard rather than those Fathers and scholastics who give men some part in their own election. The dread decree (*decretum horribile*) of reprobation is to be accepted, not investigated. It is an incomprehensible mystery before which, with Paul, "we stand astonished"; but it is not to be thought of as impugning the justice of God. The will of God is the supreme rule of righteousness. Many are called, but only the elect are effectually called, to salvation. Calvin uses chiefly Old Testament and Pauline passages in giving scriptural support to this doctrine, and he argues away the bearing upon it of certain passages which seem at variance from it. Undoubtedly he felt certain that the doctrine was soundly scriptural. It exhibits his constant rejection of every suggestion that anything can take place which God has not determined. In a chapter on the resurrection, with which Book

III is concluded, Calvin portrays in spiritual terms the felicity and glory of the redeemed, and holds that the language used in Scripture to describe the state of the damned is figurative, presenting "corporeal images" of that wretchedness which consists in alienation from God.

VI

Following the sequence of the clauses of the Creed, Calvin comes in Book IV to the exposition of "the Holy Catholic Church" and "the Communion of Saints." These expressions both refer to the entire membership of the Church of God, departed, living and unborn. This holy Church is known to God alone. The visible Church is also Catholic, though marred by imperfections. It is recognizable by two marks (*notae*): the true preaching and reverent hearing of the Word, and the right administration of the sacraments. To these Calvin adds the discipline by which they are maintained. Where these are present we may not depart from the Church's communion; to do so is to renounce God. No visible church is wholly without blemishes; and Christians are warned against a schismatic and censorious spirit. Where the marks of the Church are lacking, separation is required. The reference here is to the Roman communion; within it, however, some remnant of the true Church has persisted.

Calvin sets forth a doctrine of the ministry, in which he argues that bishops and presbyters were originally one. Besides these ministers of the Word there are those (elders) charged with discipline, and deacons who provide for and administer poor relief. Calvin, however, judges favorably the early development of the episcopate, and even justifies the offices of metropolitan bishops and patriarchs in the early Church. He dates the defection of the clergy after the time of Gregory the Great (d. 604), when the rule of the Roman

see was established on unwarranted claims (IV, vii, 17, 18).
About four chapters (v–viii) are devoted to a castigation of
the later hierarchical claims and practices. Of the ecumenical
councils Calvin writes: "I venerate them from my heart."
But they did not in all things exhibit the direction of the
Holy Spirit; and later councils have shown greater faults.

The power of the Church in legislation and jurisdiction,
and the importance and nature of discipline, are somewhat
amply treated. Discipline is likened to the ligaments (*pro
nervis est*) (IV, xii, 1) that hold the body together; the
figures of the bridle, the spur and the rod are also used. It is
useful to prevent scandal, to avoid corruption and to secure
the repentance of wrongdoers. Calvin favors "assembling,
weeping and fasting" during calamities which express God's
wrath. His opposition to clerical and monastic vows has
special reference to the clergy and monks of his time, and is
tempered by the recognition that the Church of the age of
Chrysostom obtained her ministers from the monasteries,
and that Augustine in discussing the labor of monks describes a monasticism that is "holy and legitimate" (IV, xiii,
8, 10).

Calvin expounds at length the sacraments of baptism and
the Holy Supper (IV, xiv–xvii). The sacraments are testimonies of God's grace and, on our part, badges of fidelity.
In them God accommodates Himself to our capacity, by a
visible representation of spiritual blessings. As seals confirm
documents, they confirm the Scriptures. Calvin's whole doctrine is such as to subordinate the sacraments to the Word.
They are to be accompanied by intelligible explanations, not
magical incantations. They are valueless without the work
of the Spirit in our own hearts. Baptism replaces circumcision, just as the Jewish ceremonies in general were shadows
of things deferred to be fully manifested in Christ. It is an
initiation into the fellowship of those regenerated in Christ.

Its administration is rightly confined to the public ministers of the Church. The baptism by laymen and women resorted to where infants are about to die is unjustified, since "God adopts our infants as his children before they are born," as Abraham was assured in the words "thy seed after thee" (Genesis 17:10). But pedobaptism is defended not only on the basis of circumcision in the Covenant of God with Abraham, but also from New Testament texts such as, "The promise is unto you. and to your children" (Acts 2:39). Christ commanded that the children should be brought to Him. God's grace does not wait for infants to grow to maturity; John the Baptist was sanctified before he was born; and we must not deny that some who die in infancy have in a measure received the illumination of faith. To adduce against infant baptism the passage, "Except a man be born of water and of the Spirit, he cannot enter into the kingdom of God" (John 3:5) is to adjudge all the unbaptized to eternal death. We do not deprive children of food because of the text, "If any would not work, neither should he eat" (II Thessalonians 3:10).

Calvin's doctrine of the Lord's Supper is one of participation and not merely of remembrance. He devotes to it a long chapter here (IV, xvii), and to this he adds an animated attack on the Roman doctrine of the Mass and a discussion of the ceremonies alleged to be sacraments: confirmation, penance, extreme unction, ordination and matrimony. In other writings, notably his *Little Treatise on the Holy Supper* (1541), he further expounds this doctrine. In the Supper the Holy Spirit mysteriously unites us with the heavenly body of Christ. It is not a mere "sign"; the thing signified is truly present. That the symbols used should remain bread and wine after consecration is necessary in order that they should be valid symbols. Calvin has a high view of the sacrament, however; it means "a true and substantial communication of the body and blood of the Lord." He does not employ Luther's idea of the ubiquity of Christ's resurrection body, but develops a concept that is scarcely less difficult, which has for its starting point the location in heaven of the Lord's body. The body becomes present in the sacrament through the surpassing and mysterious power of the Holy Spirit to unite things spatially separated. Calvin does not pretend to clarify the mystery. "I rather experience than understand it," he says. The religious value of his doctrine may be said to be in two points of emphasis. One is his insistence upon participation in Christ, whose life is "imfused" into us in the sacrament through the efficacy of the Spirit. Calvin here uses the language of the mystics: "Christ becomes wholly one with us and we with him." The other is his emphasis on the fellowship of all communicants in the one bread composed of many grains—a conception stressed in the early Church. This intimacy of communion makes it impossible for us to wound or despise our brethren without injuring Christ or to love Christ without loving Him in our brethren (IV, xvii, 10, 32, 38).

In the final chapter of the *Institutes* (IV, xx) Calvin leaves the strict field of theology to expound his views on civil government. It is a vividly written compendium of political doctrine. The attitude to government is highly respectful. The authority of rulers and the obedience of subjects are the basic assumptions. Calvin votes not for popular rule, nor yet for monarchy, but for a spread of responsibility among the most capable—"aristocracy mixed with democracy." He has, however, little preference for any form of government provided that it secures to the citizens a regulated liberty durably established. Magistrates hold an exalted office. They are vicegerents of God in temporal government and are obligated to rule with justice, according to law, to protect their subjects and to use their revenues economically, remembering that taxes are as the blood of the people. The public laws ought to be in accord with the eternal moral law, that is, the natural law engraved on all men's minds by God. Nations are free to frame their own laws, having regard always to "the perpetual rule of love." Under tyrannous rulers the private Christian has only to obey and to implore divine deliverance. But God often raises up public avengers of the oppressed: "Let princes hear and fear." Furthermore, where there are magistrates constitutionally appointed to protect the people and limit the power of the king, such as the ephors of Sparta, the Roman tribunes or the Athenian demarchs, these are solemnly obligated to resist the oppressor and preserve the liberty of the people. Here Calvin, in a few pregnant sentences, instituted a tradition without knowing it—the Calvinist espousal of limited monarchy, often leading to republicanism, in modern political history. It is not without significance that in the last paragraph of the treatise we read this warning: "The Israelites are condemned for having been too submissive to the impious edict of their king." The sons of Calvin have not been too submissive!

VII

We cannot here engage in an extended critical evaluation of this classical treatise in which an exceptionally gifted mind finds mature expression. Our purpose has been to follow the movement of Calvin's thought as it flows like a rapid river through a wide domain, and we have not halted to express applause or blame. It may be permitted here, however, to hold the work in retrospect for a moment. While not without minor inconsistencies, the treatise as a whole is knit together in a logical coherence rarely surpassed. Yet it is frankly theological and unphilosophical, and the author is unashamed when he closes off an area from speculation and leaves it to the realm of the mysterious. The authority is not reason but the voice of God as found in Scripture. Yet the rational faculty of the reader is constantly evoked, and no one can peruse the work without great stimulus to his reasoning powers. Thus the most scriptural of theologians has contributed to the rise of rationalism.

In many of Calvin's pages there are marks of genius that no brief résumé of them can convey. As a rhetorician Calvin was of the school of Cicero. Like Cyprian of Carthage, he learned more than rhetoric from this master, but his chief debt lies in the quality of his style. His most impressive passages have a distinctly oratorical form, and like other persuasive orators he does not hesitate to repeat in variant phraseology his favorite ideas. Unhappily, it may be said of Calvin as has been said of Cicero that "he dearly loved a bitter jest." His humor is often caustic, and he has an aptitude for turning an anecdote upon an opponent. In controversial sections he sometimes exhibits the rich vocabulary of abuse typical of much humanist writing. He yields too much to the temptation that besets clever men to display their resources of sarcasm. His vituperation is no doubt good of its kind; but it mars a work undertaken on a lofty plane, and could have been eliminated with advantage. Fortunately, great stretches of the text are free from this defect. We see the stamp of immortal literature in the burning and exalted eloquence with which he treats the sublimity and beauty of the created world, the orderly revolutions of the stars, and man with his thoughts that range through time and space and aspire toward the divine. The urgent and awe-stricken passages on the devastation wrought by sin, on the deserved wrath, undeserved mercy and sovereign majesty of God, and on the Christian life energized by faith and laden with duties, are not read to be forgotten.

It is generally admitted that historically the *Institutes* is a work of creative importance. Such a book ought not to be judged by an arbitrary selection from among its teeming ideas. Unfortunately, Calvin has suffered from both friendly and hostile interpreters who have fixed attention upon the most forbidding and most disputable sections of the treatise. It is the present writer's hope that the reader will obtain from this sketch some fresh awareness of the proportions of the work as a whole. On a comprehensive view the harsh and sub-Christian elements that are discoverable in it will be seen to be relatively insignificant, and will not greatly impair the effect of its inspiring greatness and power.

RICHARD HOOKER:

The Laws of Ecclesiastical Polity

Chapter III

RICHARD HOOKER:
The Laws of Ecclesiastical Polity

THE most valuable collection of the works of Richard
Hooker is the one "arranged" by the celebrated John Keble
and first published in 1836. The seventh edition of Keble's
Hooker, with corrections by R. W. Church and Francis
Paget, appeared in 1888.[1] It is in three large volumes. The
treatise *Of the Laws of Ecclesiastical Polity* extends from
the end of the introductory matter of Volume I beyond the
middle of Volume III. It is hardly too much to say that every
paragraph of this long work is written with distinction. It is
the crowning literary expression of the English Reformation and holds a high place in the entire history of theological writing. The title suggests more of special attention to
church polity than the work itself exhibits. Virtually the
entire field of theology is embraced within it. But Hooker's
approach and the structure of his treatise are determined by
the necessity of defending the polity of Elizabethan Anglicanism and its relation to the state, at a time when the
Elizabethan Settlement came under the criticism of Puritans
who advocated the discipline of Geneva.

Dr. Keble included with Hooker's *Works* the *Life* written by Isaak Walton in 1665. From the standpoint of wit

[1] *The Works of That Learned and Judicious Divine, Mr. Richard
Hooker* (New York: Oxford University Press, 1888), 3 vols.

and interest, it is one of Walton's choicest short biographies. Unfortunately it has been shown to be exceedingly inaccurate and at some points gravely misleading. It was based not only upon documents but also upon inquiries made by Walton among the friends and relatives of Hooker. Walton wrote it when he was more than seventy years of age and may have been provided with unverified material in order to produce a desired impression.[2] Yet some of his facts and dates are not assailed. Hooker was born in or near Exeter, in or about 1553, and died at Bishopsbourne in Kent, November 2, 1600. As a boy his excellent talents brought him to the favorable attention of John Jewel, Bishop of Salisbury, the renowned author of the *Apology for the Anglican Church,* 1562. Jewel showed him much kindness and helped him financially. On one occasion he lent the young man, who was starting out on a visit to his home, what Jewel called "the horse which hath carried me many a mile." This was the walking stick which Jewel, who was lame, had used on long trips on the Continent when he was among those in exile during Mary's reign. Hooker's work was to be, like Jewel's, a defense of Anglican principles, but whereas Jewel's opponents were Roman Catholics, Hooker's were chiefly Puritans. When Jewel wrote his *Apology* the Council of Trent was nearing the completion of its labors, and the papal cause, with its possibilities of political danger to Elizabeth, was in the ascendant. When Hooker's treatise was in preparation, the death of Mary Stuart, the defeat of the Spanish Armada and the rise of Puritan parties had changed the situation for Anglicanism. Another front had now to be defended.

Jewel died in 1571, before Hooker had given proof of his

[2] C. J. Sisson, *The Judicious Marriage of Mr. Hooker and the Birth of the Laws of Ecclesiastical Polity* (Cambridge: University Press, 1940), pp. xii–xiv, *passim.*

powers. Hooker's description of Jewel as "the worthiest divine that Christendom hath bred for the space of some hundreds of years" (*Laws of Ecclesiastical Polity*, II, vi, 4) may be a filial exaggeration; but it may justly remind us that the reformed Church of England had at least one very able theologian before Hooker. Jewel was a personal friend of Peter Martyr Vermigli and of Henry Bullinger and other Reformed theologians. At Corpus Christi College, Oxford, Hooker was exposed to the doctrines of Calvin's *Institutes* as presented by the learned Puritan John Rainolds, his tutor and friend. For reasons not clearly known, both Rainolds and Hooker, with three other fellows of the College, were expelled in 1579 by the vice president, John Barfoote, but almost immediately restored. Barfoote was hostile to Puritanism, and was at odds with Rainolds. There is some evidence that Rainolds was consulted on Books I–V of the *Laws*.[3]

At nineteen Hooker became tutor to two talented boys. One was the son of Jewel's friend and former fellow exile, Edwin Sandys, Archbishop of York, and was to be known as Sir Edwin Sandys, author of the *Speculum Europae*, 1629. The other was George Cranmer, grandson of a brother of Archbishop Cranmer. Both remained through life greatly devoted to their able tutor. Walton represents the youthful scholar as a model of piety and kindliness. If his statement is correct that in four years Hooker was absent from chapel only twice, he must have had remarkable health as well. Walton speaks of his great bashfulness and his weak sight. He also admiringly plays up the gentleness, moderation and forbearance of Hooker's disposition, even his "dovelike simplicity" when the victim of slander; but Keble is of the opinion that these qualities were his not by gift of nature but by the exercise of "unwearied self-control." Several early

[3] Cf. Keble's edition, III, 109: "D. Raynoldes [*sic*] note on the former books."

writers apply to him the epithet "judicious," on which J. W. Allen remarks that it is "almost ludicrously inadequate."[4]

II

In one important matter Walton would have us suppose that Hooker was sadly injudicious. His marriage, as Walton represents it, might be taken as material for an argument in favor of sacerdotal (or, shall we say, academic?) celibacy. According to this account, he was persuaded by a designing mother to marry her daughter. Walton remarks on the "wheel within the wheel" of Ezekiel, the strange providence that "allows not good wives to good men." It appears, however, on new evidence presented by C. J. Sisson, that Joan Churchman, Mrs. Richard Hooker, was not the heartless and parasitic wife Walton would have us think. In Walton's story, when his aristocratic pupils visited the family at his parish of Drayton in Buckinghamshire, she called Richard "to rock the cradle." Walton seems to feel that this was a crowning indignity. But the whole account is a tissue of error. We can only suppose that someone has been spoofing good old Walton. Not only were all of Hooker's six children yet unborn at the date given for the incident (1584); the parents were not married until about four years later (February 13, 1588). Hooker had been appointed to the parish of Drayton but he did not reside there. He was, in fact, residing in the home of John Churchman, father of the future Mrs. Hooker, in Watling Street. Churchman was not, as Walton says, the needy keeper of a lodginghouse, but a prosperous and honored citizen who became, in 1594, Master of the Merchant Taylors' Company. It was Hooker who

[4] *A History of Political Thought in the Sixteenth Century* (New York: Dial Press, 1928), p. 184.

was poor, and who gained in his worldly status by the marriage. After Hooker's death, his by then aged father-in-law met with impoverishing losses through ventures in troubled Ireland and abroad; but he retained the respect of all who knew him. There is no evidence that he was a partisan of the Puritans; on the contrary he was in good favor in church circles.[5]

Whether the Hooker children were rocked in the cradle by their eminent father or not, the two of them who were boys died in infancy; the four daughters survived him. The youngest of them, Margaret (Walton fails to note that at the time of her father's death she was only seven years old), became the wife of Ezekiel Chark, a minister of Puritan persuasion. The major misinformation by which Walton blackens the memory of Joan Hooker is that he places her under grave suspicion of having been a party, along with Mr. Chark, to the destruction of the finished manuscript of the last three books of the *Laws of Ecclesiastical Polity* immediately after the author's death. Of this more presently.

It was after Hooker became Master of the Temple (1585) and had as his associate Walter Travers, a strong advocate of a Presbyterian system for the Church of England, that he gave the direction to his studies that was to make him the great exponent of Anglicanism. Travers was already afternoon lecturer in the Temple church. "The pulpit," says Thomas Fuller, "spake pure Canterbury in the morning, and Geneva in the afternoon." Soon there was a keen controversy. However, each contestant showed high personal respect for the other. To inquirers Hooker called Travers "a good man," while Travers went so far as to say that Hooker was "a holy man." In this controversy the fundamental treatise we are to consider may have been conceived.

[5] Sisson, *op. cit.*, pp. 18–40.

Hooker was appointed rector of Boscombe near Salisbury in 1591, but apparently held the benefice *in absentia*.[6] Book I of the work was published in 1593. Volumes II to V appeared after his appointment to Bishopsbourne near Canterbury. All the while, however, his studies were carried on in London. Walton holds that "he hastened his own death by hastening to give life to his Books," and this is not unlikely. After the appearance of Book V in 1597 he apparently labored ardently on the remaining three books by which he intended to complete the work; but none of these had been published at the time of his death, and it is not certain how much of the work of revision had been accomplished. Walton would have us suppose that our texts of Books VI, VII and VIII are not to be regarded as authentic works of Hooker but as reconstructions based on fragmentary remainders of his notes, the completed manuscripts left by him having been destroyed or misappropriated by Chark. This view was pointedly questioned by the historian, Henry Hallam, and by Samuel Taylor Coleridge, whose *Literary Remains* contains the suggestion that Walton's "strange blind story" lacks all corroboration, and that since Walton makes much of Hooker's late intimate friendship with Adrian Saravia, this high churchman and not the Puritan relatives had to do with the disappearance of the originals.[7]

It was not until 1648 that Book VI, as we have it, and the major part of Book VIII appeared. Book VII was to wait still longer, being printed in 1662. The modern discussion of the history of the manuscripts left by Hooker, from which Books VI, VII and VIII of the work were later published, is far too technical and involved to be reviewed here. But

---

[6] *Ibid.*, p. 45.

[7] *The Literary Remains of Samuel Taylor Coleridge,* edited by H. N. Coleridge (London, 1838), III, 19 f. The passage is quoted by Sisson, *op. cit.*, pp. 186 f.

some attempt must be made to report on the outcome of the discussion. One notable contribution is that of Dr. R. A. Houk, whose chief interest is in Book VIII. Dr. Houk discards the legend of the wanton destruction of the manuscripts. He holds that the entire work was left virtually complete by Hooker and adopts the view that the publication of the series was halted because Lord Burghley was dissatisfied with Hooker's treatment of the royal prerogative. Certain points raised by Houk tend to lay at the door of Bishop Lancelot Andrewes some responsibility for the protracted delay in publication. He further points to the association of Archbishop Ussher, a man celebrated for his irenical spirit, with the publication of the eighth book in 1648. Its appearance at a late stage of Charles I's downfall was apparently expected to aid in the creation of a moderate view of royal power that might become the basis of compromise.[8]

More recently Professor Sisson has presented a body of fresh evidence, from sources previously neglected, which completely shatters the invented story set down by Walton and exonerates Joan Hooker of all blame. We know that by her husband's will she was appointed sole executrix, her father and Edwin Sandys being associated with her as "overseers" of the will. These three shared the charge of the manuscripts, and Sisson finds proof that "all had the best intentions." He reduces the difficulty of accounting for the delay by new evidence from Court of Chancery records of the suits brought by Hooker's daughters to secure legacies from the estate. There is, for example, the curious request of John Spenser, President of Corpus Christi College, Oxford, who had been entrusted with the task of editing the manu-

---

[8] R. A. Houk, *Hooker's Laws of Ecclesiastical Polity, Book VIII*, with an Introduction (New York: Columbia University Press, 1931), pp. 44-59, 86, 91-96, 108, 111 f., 116 ff.

scripts, in his testimony before the court in 1611, that he be permitted to keep silence on the reasons for his failure to have the remaining books published. Sisson shows that this was not unconnected with the difference between Edwin Sandys and Bishop Andrewes regarding matters treated in the extant part of Book VI. He holds that Hooker had out-grown the low-church views of Sandys and George Cranmer, his old pupils from whom he received comments on a part of Book VI dealing with lay elders. His view that these men favored good relations with Geneva and wished Hooker to show more pronounced hostility to Rome may be correct; but he has not shown adequate evidence of their real divergence from Hooker. Nor is this apparent from the comments referred to (published in Keble's edition, III, 108–139) when they are viewed as a whole. (In his reference to George Cranmer's proposal to hold a "politique conference" with Geneva, Sisson omits to indicate that the proposal was accompanied by suggestions, consonant with Hooker's view, of arguments to confute the lay-eldership principle.) Most of the notes of both critics express only ecclesiastically neutral details—of style, historical accuracy and adequate annotation. But no text of this part of Hooker's Book VI has survived. Sisson suggests that Sandys was responsible for its suppression and he credits Andrewes with having secured the survival (not, we note, the publication) of the other part, the so-called "Tract of Confession," now referred to as Book VI. All this fails to clarify the story in full, but it casts some light upon what it was that John Spenser was concealing in 1611.

The modern investigators are reassuring on the substantial authenticity of the last three books. Sisson defends Book VII on the question of style from doubts raised by Keble. Houk includes in his dissertation an edition of Book VIII, from the

⁹ Sisson, *op. cit.*, pp. 79–105.

Dublin manuscript which he selects as the most complete and probably nearest to Hooker's first draft. Our references to Book VIII will be to Houk's text.

III

Hooker's long Preface is an essential part of the treatise. It is addressed "to them that seek the reformation of laws and orders ecclesiastical in the Church of England." These are the Puritans, especially the Presbyterians such as Walter Travers and Thomas Cartwright, and the authors of the abusive Marprelate Tracts (1588). The foundation of their discipline comes from Calvin, who is described as "incomparably the wisest man that the French Church did enjoy, since the hour it enjoyed him." That this phrase is, as some have supposed, designedly ambiguous, seems unlikely from much that follows. Thousands were indebted to Calvin: he was indebted not to human teachers but to God, author of the Book of Life and of that dexterity of wit and of those helps of learning with which the French reformer was endowed. Hooker treats the history of Geneva vividly, critically and withal respectfully. He approves Calvin's plan of Church government, in view of the vacancy of authority resulting from the flight of the bishop:

This device, I see not how the wisest at this time living could have bettered, if we duly consider what the present estate of Geneva did then require (Preface, ii, 4).

Calvin's action in establishing the discipline he finds more commendable than Calvin's claims of divine (scriptural) authority in support of it. The enormous growth of Calvin's influence has resulted in the attempt of some of his recent disciples to supplant the discipline of other churches by that of Geneva. Hooker leads on to the English Presbyterians, and cites their Admonitions to Parliament (of 1572) and

Cartwright's defense of these. Cartwright was a well-known man: he had been in a running conflict with John Whitgift, who was now archbishop of Canterbury. Whitgift had not the learning, or the time, to answer him effectively. Hooker is entering the lists against him; but we should remember that Cartwright is already personally reconciled to Whitgift, and is now only by what he has written a dangerous opponent. Here occurs what is probably Hooker's most frequently quoted sentence:

> Concerning the Defender of which Admonitions, all that I mean to say is but this: *there will come a time when three words uttered with charity and meekness shall receive a far more blessed reward than three thousand volumes written with disdainful sharpness of wit* (Preface, ii, 10).

The passage, of course, carries a powerful rebuke to the now aging Cartwright, who had indeed sometimes written with disdainful wit. Hooker habitually avoids this manner of writing. In his most insistent arguments he is considerate, charitable and good-tempered, a model to all theologians. When he remonstrates with his opponents he sometimes allows himself a little amusement at their expense:

> Yet we are not able to define whether the wisdom of God . . . might not permit those worthy vessels of his glory [Luther and Calvin] to be in some things blemished with the stain of human frailty, even for this cause, lest we should esteem of any man above that which behoveth (Preface, iv, 8).

This is the effective satire of understatement, but the mood is not "disdainful."

What has been said will indicate something of Hooker's orientation. His mind has been represented as chiefly under medieval influences. The degree in which this is the case with the Continental reformers renders questionable the sharp contrast drawn by some interpreters between him and them. Certainly he accepts the Reformation in its Anglican manifestation, and has no thought of undoing its work. Since for him the Reformation is in the past, he is not himself a "reformer." In a general way he is not unfavorable to Continental Protestantism. Even the Genevan discipline is moderately approved—as discipline for Geneva. But the Church of England has been reformed, and does not need the application of the Genevan discipline as the would-be "reformers" now vocal in England demand. Hooker likes the Church of England as she is, and wants no remodeling of her structure. He will admit that she might be improved, but within the system essentially as it exists.

IV

Keble unaccountably represents Hooker as having checked the trend to rationalism in the Anglicanism of his time.[10] In the light of more modern interpretations of Hooker, and indeed of the evidence of the work itself, he is rather to be classified as the primary inspirer of the rationalistic approach to theology and ecclesiology. This statement is borne out by the entire content of Book I as well as by many passages in the other books. Hooker is summoning the mind of the reader to a judicial view of the problems of Church law and Church order. It is a part of his strategy against the spokesmen of Puritanism to maintain a tone of objectivity and rationality and not to adopt too explicitly the method of the pleader for a cause. His opponents have proposed alterations in the structure of the Church and in its rules and discipline. These projected reforms lie within the field of law. Hooker begins by a philosophical examination of the problem of law and of the law of God, reaching to generalizations that cut away the basic principles of the Puritan assailants of Anglicanism.

[10] *Op. cit.*, I, cxv.

Behold therefore we offer the laws whereby we live unto the general trial and judgment of the whole world; heartily beseeching Almighty God, whom we desire to serve according to his own will, that both we and others (all kind of partial affection being clean laid aside) may have eyes to see and hearts to embrace the things that in his sight are most acceptable (I, i, 3).

Hooker points to the fact that wise and learned heathens have acknowledged some first cause of all things and ascribed to this first cause intellect and reason. They err who think that there is no reason for God's will to do this or that. The reason may not be known to us but it is in the "counsel of his own will" (Ephesians 1:11). The divine reason suffuses the divine law; and although God's law is immutable, the freedom of his will is not thereby hindered. Hooker's categories of eternal, natural, divine and human law correspond to those of Thomas Aquinas and are, in fact, commonplace among theologians who treat of this subject. He lays great emphasis upon the law of nature and, as already indicated, upon the law of reason which "bindeth creatures reasonable in this world."

When Hooker speaks of the "law of nature," he is primarily thinking of the regular and uninterrupted series of movements and acts that are found in material nature and in the animal world. With reference to man he commonly uses the term "law of reason." In some respects Hooker's thought lies close to that of Christopher St. German (d. 1540), the able jurist of the reign of Henry VIII, who usually employs the term "law of reason" where other authors would commonly use "law of nature." The law of nature in Hooker's application of it is, of course, no less than the law of reason, a law of God, and represents "an authentical or an original draught written in the bosom of God himself" (I, iii, 4).

Hooker rises from the theme of law in the natural world

to law in the world of intellectual beings, distinguishing therein angels from men. Men differ from the angels in the degree of knowledge of which they are by nature possessed. Men begin life with no knowledge and acquire it only in limited degree. Men are distinct from the beasts in that the soul of man is capable of reaching "higher than unto sensible things." Hooker, however, gives no encouragement to man's insatiable curiosity and seems to feel that it is particularly necessary in the age in which he lives ("this present age full of tongue and weak of brain") to avoid too exalted efforts of reason and research (I, viii, 2).

Hooker teaches a doctrine of freedom of the will. In the processes of nature, choice is not possible. The fire cannot choose but to consume the stubble; but man has knowledge and will. Choice is the will tending toward any end. In things that require understanding, reason is the director of man's will, and the laws of well-doing are the dictates of right reason. Children and madmen may not exercise free choice since in them reason is undeveloped or absent. But Hooker recognizes that the will is drawn aside by appetite which disinclines it to do what reason enjoins. Reason may discern what is good and the will fail to choose it.

In the discussion of the way of finding out by reason laws to guide the will, Hooker indicates his agreement with the old law maxim, *Vox populi, vox Dei,* which he improves by translating: "The general and perpetual voice of man is as the sentence of God himself." This is true in the sense that what men have at all times learned, nature herself must have taught as the instrument of God. Man has to obey the rule that reason gives concerning the goodness of actions to be done. According to Hooker, the law in the general sense is "the directive rule unto goodness of operation." Again, he says: "But the nature of Goodness being thus ample, a Law is properly that which Reason in such sort defineth to be good that it must be done." Laws of reason, moreover, may be investigated by reason without the help of revelation, and they are such that the knowledge of them is general among men. In this connection Hooker quotes the well-known lines of Sophocles, often cited by historians of natural law: "It is no child of today's or yesterday's birth, 'but hath been no man knoweth how long sithence.' "[11] In further exposition of Hooker's view of the law of nature let us quote:

> Law rational therefore, which men commonly use to call the Law of Nature, meaning thereby the Law which human Nature knoweth itself in reason universally bound unto, which also for that cause may be termed most fitly the Law of Reason; this Law, I say, comprehendeth all those things which men by the light of their natural understanding evidently know, or at least-wise may know, to be beseeming or unbeseeming, virtuous or vicious, good or evil for them to do (I, viii, 9).

Undoubtedly Hooker has a high view of man's endowment of reason. Nevertheless, like other theologians, he sees the limitations of natural law with respect to human virtue and is as much aware as Calvin (though not so insistent on the point) that man and all creatures are dependent upon the continual help of God. "There is no kind of faculty or power in man or any other creature, which can rightly perform the functions allotted to it, without perpetual aid and concurrence of that Supreme Cause of all things." In contrast to the lower ceatures, man, by his obedience to or violation of the law of nature or of reason, is capable of righteousness and of sin. Hooker, however, lays no stress upon the fact of Adam's fall in all this; instead he calls attention to the contagion of "lewd and wicked custom," and continually refers to the present action of the human will. It is recognized that man is habitually a sinner and that, without the revelation of God, he is unable to know ade-

[11] Sophocles, *Antigone*, v. 456.

quately the things that are needful for his salvation (I, viii, 11–ix, 1).

With such generalizations Hooker turns to the fact of law in government. Human laws are made under the exercise of human reason, and on the promptings of nature and reason men unite themselves into politic societies under governments. Governments arise from two foundations: the natural inclination to society and fellowship, and an agreement reached regarding the manner in which men shall live together. Thus Hooker is an exponent of the contract theory of government. This agreement he speaks of as the "Law of a Commonweal" and the very soul of the politic body. It is necessary for politic (or positive) laws to be framed on the assumption that man is in a state of depravity and that his actions may be controlled so as to avoid hindrance of the common good (I, x, 1). This is the kind of doctrine that produced the provision for "checks and balances" in the American Constitution. It is human depravity that must be checked.

The law of nature, however, does not require that any one particular form of government be adopted. The form of government is a matter of choice to be made in accordance with experience and need. But, according to Hooker, experience has shown that "to live by one man's will became the cause of all man's misery."

Natural laws bind universally: positive laws do not. Yet positive laws are of the greatest importance and should be framed by the wisest men. If they are to be revered, they must "speak with indifferency" and avoid respect of persons. The laws receive their authority, however, not from those who devise them but from the power of government. Hooker holds that the power of making laws falls under the obligations of natural law, and that the lawmakers are ultimately the entire societies in which they are enforced.

Princes may not make laws merely by a power alleged to be personally received from God. "Laws they are not, therefore, which public approbation hath not made so" (I, x, 9).

Hooker is only incidentally concerned with international law, but what he says of it is not without importance. He refers to the laws of commerce between nations, to laws concerning embassage and the entertainment of foreigners and also to the laws of war. Here he expresses the high sentiment that just as the civil law overrules each part of the state, "so there is no reason that any one commonwealth of itself should to the prejudice of another annihilate that whereupon the whole world hath agreed." In other words, international relations should be subjected to the law of nature or of reason (I, x, 13).

With his characteristic emphasis upon matters ecclesiastical, Hooker here indicates his belief that the restoration of the authority of general councils in the Church, and the frequent meetings of these, would be conducive to pacification, and to communion among Christian nations. That certain nations, including his own, are Christian, is to Hooker axiomatic.

Hooker's conception of the *summum bonum*, "our Sovereign Good or Blessedness," is that of the union of the human soul with God. It is the summit of a series of goods, and superior to those goods which are instrumental only, such as riches, and to those which, while good in themselves, are desirable only in view of a further end, such as health or knowledge. Men may perversely set as their highest good that which is not infinite. But the infinite good which is God is our ultimate felicity. By nature all men desire happiness. The present life does not provide the satisfaction of this desire.

For although the beauties, riches, honours, sciences, virtues and perfections of all men living, were in the present possession of one; yet somewhat beyond and above all this there would still be sought and earnestly thirsted for (I, xi, 4).

This fact points to man's need of a supernatural blessedness. The light of nature cannot lead us to bliss except in a limited way through the performance of duty. This is inadequate to man's higher desires. There is no entrance into blessedness without Christian belief, which is the ground of divine virtues.

It is very obvious that Hooker is following a pattern of thought very close to that of Thomas Aquinas. In a summary sentence he states the argument thus:

We see, therefore, that our sovereign good is desired naturally; that God, the author of that natural desire, had appointed natural means whereby to fulfill it; that man having utterly disabled his nature unto those means hath had other revealed from God, and hath received from heaven a law to teach him how that which is desired naturally must now supernaturally be attained (I, xii, 3).

Hooker concerns himself with the problem of Scripture and tradition. He values tradition, but finds it hopelessly inadequate and inferior to Scripture. We should be in a miserable state if we had to depend upon the memory of man for the law of God. Scripture abounds with all sorts of laws but its principal purpose is "to deliver the laws of duty supernatural." Hooker discussses its adequacy to do this, and concludes that the Scriptures are the articles of God sufficient to lay before us all the duties which God requires.

V

Hooker has established, in the course of his argument in Book I, the crowning importance of law, and the continuity of the Church with the state in relation to the divine law. The Church and state are distinguished, yet united.

The Church being a supernatural society doth differ from natural societies in this, that the persons unto whom we associate ourselves in the one are men simply considered as men, but they to whom we be joined in the other, are God, Angels, and holy men (I, xv, 2).

Toward the end of the book he defends his method of approaching the topic of ecclesiastical law from the point of view of a general discussion of laws, even though a contrary method might have been "more popular and more plausible to vulgar ears." He has sought in this first book, as he tells us, to teach men why just and reasonable laws are of so great force and of so great use in the world. At the end of the book he has this eloquent and typical sentence:

Of Law there can be no less acknowledged, than that her seat is the bosom of God, her voice the harmony of the world: all things in heaven and earth do her homage, the very least as feeling her care, and the greatest as not exempted from her power, both Angels and men and creatures of what condition soever, though each in different sort and manner, yet all with uniform consent admiring her as the mother of their peace and joy (I, xvi, 8).

We may believe that Hooker consciously put his best effort into this first section of his great work. It is in itself a treatise of independent value. It is also a very able introduction to the attack he is about to make upon the Puritan enemies of the Anglican establishment, challenging as it does the reader's sense of fairness and arousing in him, should he be capable of it, a philosophical and judicial frame of mind. We may here refer to a story, without assuming it to be authentic, which is recorded by Walton. According to this tale the English Roman Catholic, Dr. Stapleton, read the first book of the laws in oral translation to Pope Clement VIII, and the pope was so impressed as to remark: "There is no learning that this man hath not searcht into . . . his books will get reverence by age for there is in them such seeds of eternity that if the rest be like this, they shall last till the last fire shall consume all learning."[12]

VI

Any reader familiar with Hooker's great work recognizes at once that Book VIII bears a close relation to Book I. Something will be gained of understanding if we turn now to this final book of the treatise. The eighth book is a strong apologetic for the Elizabethan Settlement of Anglicanism. Here Hooker proceeds to discuss the relation of Church and state. He carefully distinguishes the Church from the state while at the same time identifying, so far as England is concerned, the membership of the two societies.

There is not any man of the Church of England but the same man is also a member of the commonwealth; nor any man a member of the commonwealth which is not also of the Church of England.

While the one lives under spiritual and the other under secular law, they are "personally one society" (VIII, i, 2, 4). His insistence upon this principle is required by the arguments of his opponents who are seeking a discipline involving excommunication and the autonomy of the Church in relation to the state. Obviously Hooker is here not exactly reporting the facts of the situation. Everybody knew that there were nonconformists of one group and another in the England of Hooker's time. There were members of the commonwealth who had abandoned membership in the national church. But these were not yet so numerous as greatly to disturb the general pattern of conformity which the existing laws of England were designed to produce.

With regard to excommunication, he points out that "it

[12] Walton, *Life*. Keble, *op. cit.*, I, 71.

cutteth off indeed from the Church, and yet not from the commonwealth." The excommunicated man is not thus really severed from the body of persons with whom he is associated in Church and state alike. A man may be excommunicated and also deprived of civil dignity; after which he may be reunited to one but not to the other of the two societies. In Book III he puts the argument otherwise: excommunication does not exclude from the mystical Church, nor even completely from the visible. Hooker's extended treatment of this point, chiefly developed in the eighth book, indicates that the Church's power to exclude from its membership is limited, and that the ruler is not censurable in Church courts. Under the dominion of unbelievers, the Church and commonwealth were totally independent. In those commonwealths that are under Roman obedience, one society is both Church and commonwealth. But within the realm of England neither of these conditions obtains. "Our church hath dependency upon the chief in our commonwealth." This he believes is "in accord with the pattern of God's own ancient elect people" (III, i, 13; VIII, ii, ix).

The eighth book also treats at some length the question of secular government, with special attention to the authority of the king. Hooker commends highly the wisdom of those who laid the foundations of the English system, for the fact that they subjected everyone to the king and yet limited the king's power over all his subjects by the authority of law. He here cites the English axiom, *Lex facit regem*, a phrase which can also be duplicated in the *Vindiciae contra Tyrannos* (1579) and other writings of French Protestant publicists before Hooker. He may have been stimulated, too, by John Ponet's *Short Treatise of Politike Power* (1556).[13] But

[13] The point is raised by W. S. Hudson, *John Ponet, Advocate of Limited Monarchy* (Chicago: University of Chicago Press, 1942), pp. 206 ff.

he is decidedly more of a monarchist than these writers, and
it is actually in course of a defense of the royal prerogative
that he lays down the limits of royal authority. Indeed, his
assertion of a veto power in the Crown is an element of
royal absolution itself.[14]

With regard to the source of law for the Church, Hooker
is nearer to Marsiglio of Padua than to Thomas Aquinas. All
free and independent societies, he tells us, should make their
own laws.

> For if the commonwealth be Christian, if the people which are
> of it do publicly embrace the true religion, this very thing doth
> make it the church, as hath been shewed" (VIII, vi, 6).

Thus the making of laws for the Church does not reside
with the clergy as an autonomous body but with that body
which is (representatively) both Church and commonwealth—"the parliament of England, together with the con-
vocation annexed thereunto." He thinks of Parliament here
as including the sovereign: Sir John Fortescue's phrase (*ca.*
1470) had been "the king in Parliament." In the lost part of
Book VI, Hooker evidently wrote something in refutation
of Erastus. But he is a representative of a cautious Erastianism. To defend the Church of Elizabeth's England he had to
take that position. The secular power has a large part in reg-
ulating the Church, and "parliament is not so merely temporal as if it might meddle with nothing but leather and
wool." In Queen Mary's time, he shrewdly observes, it took
action to restore papal sway in England, and Cardinal Pole
did not think this a violation of the law of nature (VIII,
vi, 11).

Hooker, in accordance with Elizabeth's Act of Uniform-

[14] See the treatment of "the basis of political obligation" in
Hooker by E. T. Davies, *Political Ideas of Richard Hooker* (London:
S.P.C.K., 1946), chap. iv.

ity, which made the queen "supreme governor" in all ecclesiastical as well as temporal causes, recognizes "the King's
supereminent authority" in ecclesiastical affairs, but not in
the sense that he can dictate to the Church in matters of
worship and faith. His is a universal power over all authorities and causes in his domain, and when the whole ecclesiastical estate is in need of reform, he may institute it. His
authority remains, even if, being himself unfit to judge, he
leaves final judgment to commissions appointed under him.
Hooker assumes that Calvin was misinformed when he
judged Henry VIII's title, "Supreme Head of the Church,"
a blasphemous one, and labors to deny that the English
sovereigns exercise any authority that belongs to Christ.

In America, after a long period of separation of Church
and state, we do not take kindly to Hooker's moderate
Erastianism and his assertion of the king's power. It is well
to bear in mind that in all Europe only a small minority of
separatists in his time desired a Church unattached to the
secular government. Further, Hooker is not surrendering
religion to an irreligious lay state. This is not the secularist
type of Erastianism that we find in Hobbes. Hooker has a
very sincere regard for religious values, and for the main-
tenance of true religion.

VII

We can permit ourselves only brief reference to the remaining books of the treatise. In Books II, III and IV Hooker
engages his Puritan opponents in direct combat. Is the
Scripture, as they allege, the sole guide to our actions? The
point bears upon the question of the ceremonies in the
Church of England not authorized in Scripture. How, then,
asks Hooker, does Scripture itself extol the "wisdom" of
Solomon? And how could St. Peter ask Christians to live so

as to approve themselves to Gentiles who knew no Scripture? Cartwright has cited Cicero's principle, "That nothing ought to be done whereof thou doubtest whether it be right or wrong." Hooker adroitly notes the implied admission of wisdom in one unacquainted with Scripture. Moreover, the method of sustaining the sole authority of Scripture by quotation from it does not reach final proof. Such an argument as this would have made Calvin shudder:

For if any one book of Scripture did give testimony to all, yet still that Scripture which giveth credit to the rest would require another Scripture to give credit unto it; neither could we ever come unto any pause whereon to rest our assurance this way . . . (II, iv, 2).

Hooker learnedly wrestles with his learned opponents' use of the teaching of the Church Fathers on the authority of Scripture. He keeps up a persistent claim for reason: "one demonstrative reason" would outweigh ten thousand general councils (III, vii, 5). Scripture is perfect for the purpose for which God delivered it. It does not supersede the law of nature or the use of reason, or cancel the value of human testimony. Hooker claims to stand in a sound intermediate position between the schools of Rome, for whom Scripture without tradition is an insufficient revelation, and the Puritans, for whom every action not enjoined in Scripture is sin.

Calvin's view that Scripture is authenticated by the inward testimony of the Spirit, is not sufficient for Hooker. These workings of the Spirit are too "privy and secret": we should examine by reason what we are taught by the Spirit. Christ and the Apostles used natural reason. The Church Fathers sought to establish the authority of Scripture by rational arguments. If I believe the Gospel, reason is yet of use to confirm my belief; if I do not believe, I may be reasonably persuaded.

Against claims for a scriptural, presbyterian discipline

Hooker holds that Church polity is not a thing prescribed by Scripture. In matters not prescribed in Scripture the Church may use discretion. Laws governing the polity of the Church are mutable. Even the divinely given ceremonial laws of the Jews were impermanent. Calvin, indeed, had perceived what the Puritans deny, that the Church has power to make laws (*Institutes* IV, x, 30). Apart from those constant functions to which the Church "standeth bound"— the Word, sacraments, prayers, censures, etc.—she has freedom to frame the laws by which the way of performing these duties may be regulated.

Having thus asserted the Church's competence to make those laws of polity which go beyond Scripture, Hooker defends the Anglican ceremonies which have been assailed as unscriptural. It is charged that "our orders and ceremonies are papistical." It is one thing to "disallow those Romish ceremonies that are unprofitable" and another "to count all unprofitable which are Romish" (IV, iv, 3). Adherents of Rome are heretics; but whether they are Catholics or heretics is not the point here. A mere "affectation of dissimilitude" is no sound basis of judgment in matters in themselves indifferent. For an absolute rejection of the rites and forms of Roman Catholicism, Cartwright had invoked the maxim, "Contraries are cured by their contraries"—a medical principle frequently employed by early authors on the penitential discipline. On this Hooker's characteristic comment is:

He that will take away extreme heat by setting the body in extremity of cold, shall undoubtedly remove the disease, but together with it the diseased too (IV, viii, 1).

The right treatment, he indicates, would be to provide the contrary element in a measure conducive to a cure. In this medical analogy we have a perfect key to Hooker's mind. Let us have nothing extreme, but rather moderation and sweet reasonableness, as these are embodied in Anglicanism.

The defense in great detail of the Anglican way of worship extends through the long fifth book. This book was the subject of an ample exposition by Francis Paget,[15] and was edited with notes by Ronald Bayne.[16] Paget selects for special praise the treatment of the Eucharist in Chapter lxvii. It is a deeply religious and a truly charitable statement of this central and controverted doctrine. True, Hooker somewhat unfairly represents Zwingli as teaching a view of the sacrament "empty and void of Christ." But he regards this opinion as having been left behind in the Reformation, and discerns "a general agreement concerning that which alone is material, namely a *real participation* of Christ and of life in his body and blood *by means of this sacrament.*" Contentions about the manner of the presence are vain and unprofitable.

Take therefore that wherein we all agree, and then consider by itself what cause why the rest in question should not rather be left as superfluous than urged as necessary (V, lxvii, 7).

Hooker here states his opinion that the doctrine of those dubbed "Sacramentaries" (Calvin and Bullinger) has been "traduced" by their (Lutheran) critics. The entire book presents Anglicanism in a way inviting to the religious mind. It is the revelation of a religion both moderate and devout, and of a cultus which is the basis of a culture. The document included as an appendix to Book V deals with grace and the sacraments and contains a discussion of sin. Hooker reveals his familiarity with patristic treatments of these topics. Our fall in Adam leaves his posterity all in sin, and the merits of Christ are the sole effectual means to procure eternal life. The Church Fathers, he states, are agreed "that reprobation

[15] *Introduction to the Fifth Book of Hooker's Treatise of the Laws of Ecclesiastical Polity* (Oxford: Clarendon Press, 1899).

[16] Ronald Bayne, *Of the Laws of Ecclesiastical Polity. The Fifth Book. By Richard Hooker* (London: Macmillan, 1902).

presupposes foreseen sin" (33:35)—a view opposed by Calvin. Against the Jesuit Bellarmin's doctrine of justification he writes earlier in this treatise:

> *Remission of sins* is grace, because it is God's own free gift; faith, which qualifieth our minds to receive it is also grace, because it is an effect of his gracious spirit in us; we are therefore justified by faith without works, by grace without merit. . . . To the imputation of Christ's death for remission of sins, we teach faith alone necessary.

He remarks on the teaching of the Thomists, which makes other things than this necessary: "The Fathers have it not in their writings" (16, 17; in Bayne's edition, pp. 657 f.).

Book VI, as we have it, assails certain Roman Catholic defenders of auricular confession and, with a favorable comment on Lutheran practice in this matter, proceeds to expound the Anglican position.

Book VII is Hooker's defense of the episcopate. The defense is on "broad church" lines. Episcopacy is historical and salutary. Hooker cites Calvin's free acknowledgment that it was good for the order and discipline of the Church in the early centuries (*Institutes* VII, vi, 9; xi, 11). Episcopacy is precious; we may say it is ideally indispensable; the Scottish and French Reformed churches are defective without it. But Keble overstates the approximation to a high-church doctrine of succession in Hooker.[17] As Foakes-Jackson truly remarks, he "does not consider the institution absolutely indispensable."[18] A church without it does not for that reason cease to be a church. This is in accord with his general position in relation to the Reformation which has already been mentioned. Keble's view is that he began "from a point not far short of what may be called extreme protestantism, whence he moved to higher views asserting his independence and diverging from Calvinism."[19] Houk repeatedly as-

---

[17] Keble, *op. cit.*, I, lxvi–lxxxv.
[18] *Cambridge History of English Literature*, III, 414.

serts that Hooker was a Protestant, and regards him as nearer to the Lutheran than to the Calvinist position.[20] Much here depends on our choice of terms. It is safe only, and it is sufficient, to label Hooker "Anglican." As an Anglican he treats the Continental reformers with critical respect; it is to be observed that he does not include them with the Puritans in the opposition camp. He sometimes dissents from them, but he repeatedly cites Calvin against the Puritans. When he uses the word "reformers" to signify the English Presbyterian writers, he is not confusing the latter with their Continental predecessors.

VIII

This brief examination of Hooker's weighty and classical treatise has at least brought to notice some of its leading qualities. No religious writer has more appeal than Hooker to the academic reader, who, it is presumed, demands that his reason be enlisted and is alienated by everything fanatical. Hooker's rationality and liberality would, however, be insufficient to give him a continuous reading public without his mastery of a style appropriate to his message. Unlike Calvin, Hooker wrote his major work in his native language. With none of the artificial ornamentation that characterized many prose writers of the Elizabethan age, Hooker wields a facile and mighty pen, choosing his words and constructing his phrases so as to give maximum force to his arguments. His is the English of a Latin scholar. Thomas Fuller shrewdly remarked: "His stile was long and pithy, drawing on a whole flock of clauses before he came to the close of a

[19] Keble, *op. cit.*, I, lxxxviii, cx ff.

[20] Houk, *op. cit.*, pp. 70, 134–144, 153 ff. John Gauden, bishop of Exeter, in his life of Hooker published with the 1662 edition of the *Laws of Ecclesiastical Polity*, quotes (p. 38) a rhymed enconium which concludes:

> "Go read this Book; it will thee, if thou art
> True Protestant, confirm; if not, convert."

sentence." But with Hooker a long sentence is almost never a confused or blurred statement. Long or short, his sentences exactly say something that has been exactly thought. We may also call him an author who writes by ear. Rhythm and musical inflection suffuse his paragraphs and crown the passages of special eloquence. His resonant periods, syllogisms half-concealed by art, phrases at once gentle and pulverizing, and the ease, sureness and amplitude of his learning are not least among the reasons why readers of Hooker will always be his advocates. He offers, too, a retreat for rationality in this age of irrational forces—nay more, a means of recuperation for Reason herself.

The theological reader stands to profit by this. He will also be stimulated by Hooker's treatment of some of the very problems of Church government that are confronted in the progress of the ecumenical movement in contemporary Christianity. It is beyond our present purpose to set forth the views of Hooker's opponents, and a certain injustice will arise if we assume that they were mere fanatical extremists. Hooker, be it understood, does not ask us to treat them as such. It is fair to them and to him that we should say this. On the whole he is saying to them, as well as to the reader, "Come now, let us reason together." The spirit of Hooker's approach, his behavior in controversy, the moderation of his argument, no less than of the position for which he argues, have permanent lessons for the Christian mind. It is far from impossible that the future reunion of the churches of the Reformation, if it proceeds, will follow the lines of Hooker's broad-church episcopal theory. Episcopacy may be accepted as venerable and desirable without being held to be by divine authority absolutely essential. But even if he should fail to win us to agreement with him, the reading of his pages cannot fail to put us in a frame of mind in which we shall be more disposed to agree with one another.

JOHN BUNYAN:

The Pilgrim's Progress

Chapter IV

JOHN BUNYAN:
The Pilgrim's Progress

JOHN BUNYAN began life in lowly circumstances, and what formal schooling he obtained merely enabled him to read and write. His real education came through a protracted inner religious struggle, in which he suffered torment but found seasons of relief and from which he emerged a delivered soul. The fact that when out of jail he earned his living as a maker and mender of pots and kettles is of only incidental importance. Religion enlisted all the energies of his gifted mind. It controlled his interpretation of all that he observed; it sustained him through twelve years of wretched imprisonment and nourished his creative genius. His great allegories are not only fashioned by a rarely powerful imagination; they are wrought out of the stuff of his own experience. The autobiographical *Grace Abounding to the Chief of Sinners* (1666) forms the best introduction to *The Pilgrim's Progress*[1] (1678; Part II in 1685) and *The Holy War*[2] (1682), as well as to the realistic and somewhat inferior dialogue, *The Life and Death of Mr. Badman* (1680). Bunyan himself had been on an exciting and perilous pilgrimage

[1] *The Pilgrim's Progress from This World to That Which Is to Come. Delivered under the Similitude of a Dream.*

[2] *The Holy War Made by Shaddai upon Diabolus, for the Regaining of the Metropolis of the World; or The Losing and Taking Again of the Town of Mansoul.*

much like that of his hero, Christian. He had been at war, not only in the ranks of Cromwell's troopers; there had been a "holy war" within him, as within Mansoul. So, we find in *Grace Abounding* anticipations of critical scenes in the allegories. There are many such passages as these: "I found myself in a miry bog, that shook if I did but stir"; "I was often as if I had run upon the pikes"; "But oh, how Satan did now lay about him for to bring me down again!" Bunyan naturally thought in images and "similitudes," and as his experience ripened, these expanded and drew together into sustained works of allegorical fiction.

In Elstow, Bedfordshire, he grew up tall and strong and fond of sports. He pictures himself as one who in youth "had few equals" in profanity and lying. But, like Francis Thompson, he was the object of the divine pursuit. God "scared and terrified" him with dreams of hell, and voices of warning reached him among his worldly companions. His practice of ringing the bells of the parish church was now felt by him to be a dangerously sinful pleasure. While playing tipcat (a game in which a piece of wood is struck to a distance by a bat) he was arrested by a voice from heaven asking: "Wilt thou leave thy sins and go to heaven, or wilt thou have thy sins and go to hell?" He profited by the rebuke of a woman who, though herself far from saintly, charged him with spoiling the youth of the town by his swearing.

At twenty, Bunyan was married to a young woman whose sole wealth consisted of two religious books, Lewis Bayly's oft-printed *Practice of Pietie*, and Arthur Dent's *Plain Man's Pathway to Heaven*. The former prescribes an exacting routine of prayer and pious discipline; the latter is one of many books then in circulation featuring the theme of the devout pilgrimage. Reading these books, and attending church with his wife, Bunyan reformed his outward conduct, though it was long before he weaned himself from Sunday afternoon games and dancing. Once, when he had removed to Bedford to pursue his calling, he overheard the pious conversation of some poor women sitting at a door in the sun, who spoke of the new birth "as if joy did make them speak." In a vision he saw them happily situated on the sunny side of a mountain while he was in a realm of cold and clouds, separated from them by a wall. There were many such symbolic visions and dreams.

Bunyan's Pilgrim is first discovered "with a book in his hand and a great burden upon his back." In a scene that follows Mr. Worldly Wiseman asks Christian: "How camest thou by thy burden at the first?" and the reply is: "By reading this book in my hand." So it was, indeed, with the author. The Scripture convicted him of sin, while it offered the way of salvation from it. As a troubled sinner, and later as a confident preacher, he was a constant reader of the Bible. It was of unquestioned authority for him, and it had a vital message for his every mood. His habit of consulting it was his protection against the Ranters, an enthusiastic anti-Biblical sect, whose adherents he met early in his Bedford period. "The Bible," he notes, "was precious to me in those days." In fact, it equally terrified and fascinated him. How often in *Grace Abounding* does a verse of Scripture start him off on a fresh chapter of experience! "That Scripture did also tear and rend my soul, 'There is no peace, saith my God to the wicked.'" Satan could not prevail against him, he says, because "that sentence, 'this sin is not unto death,' stood as a mill-post at my back." "I was much followed by that Scripture: 'Simon, Simon, Satan hath desired to have thee?'" In the last-mentioned instance he imagined that a supernatural voice was launching the warning at him from a distance of half a mile. This happens in one of his depressions. A little while before he had been exulting in the message of his Puritan minister, John Gifford (the Evangelist of the allegory), who in concluding his sermon on the text, "Behold thou art fair, my love," had urged the tempted and anxious soul to cling to the words, "my love." Gifford's teaching, he says, helped at this period to give him "stability." Gifford was himself one of the twice-born; he had been a drunkard and a gambler. Bunyan's sins may have seemed to him pale beside his own.

Bunyan read now also Luther's *Commentary on Galatians*, which had been translated into English in 1575. He writes of this:

> I found my condition in his experience so largely and so profoundly handled, as if his book had been written out of my heart. This made me marvel. . . . I do prefer this book of Martin Luther upon the Galatians, excepting the Holy Bible, before all books that ever I have seen, as most fit for a wounded conscience. And now I found, as I thought, that I loved Christ dearly. . . . I felt my love to him as hot as fire.

But new trials were to follow. For a time it was the sin of Judas that haunted his thoughts. At every moment an evil voice prompted him to "sell Christ for this or sell Christ for that." His oft-repeated answer was, "No, no, not for thousands, thousands, thousands!" until in exhaustion he sought relief by consent, and sank into prolonged despair. Had he not sinned with that profane person, Esau, who sold his birthright and found no repentance? "These words were to my soul like fetters of brass to my legs." His sins were compared with those of Peter, David, Solomon and others whose lapses are recorded in Scripture. But light gleamed once more. When "in a most woeful state" he was pacing the floor of his cottage, "that word of God took hold of my heart: 'Ye are justified freely by his grace. . .!' " In the end, wearied and weakened by the struggle, he was borne to a new level of security by the comforting phrases that follow the disquieting Esau passage in Hebrews 12: "Ye are come unto mount Zion. . . ." It was years later, about 1655, that he began to "speak a word of exhortation," and became a preacher to those most alienated from religion.

In 1660 under Charles II he was thrust into Bedford-county jail for unlicensed preaching and because, for conscience sake, he declined to promise silence. The choice was a hard one. Some years earlier his wife had died, leaving four young children, and he had now married again. He was warmly attached to his family, especially to his afflicted daughter Mary, whom he calls "my poor blind child." It proved to be a twelve-year imprisonment. It was when this period was half spent that he wrote the personal record we have been quoting. In it he could say: "I never had in all my life so great an inlet into the Word of God as now." The "book in his hand" was his constant companion and the inspiration of all that he had to say by tongue or pen.

There have been very interesting conjectures regarding a possible influence upon Bunyan's mind of medieval allegories featuring the pilgrimage theme.[3] John Brown, in a careful biography of Bunyan,[4] pointed out some of the earlier approximations to his pilgrim story, and the subject has been

[3] J. B. Wharey, *A Study of the Sources of Bunyan's Allegories* (Baltimore: Johns Hopkins, 1904). Cf. N. Hill, *The Ancient Poem of Guillaume de Guileville Entitled Le Pèleringe de l'homme* (London: 1858) and *A Modern Prose Translation of the Ancient Poem Entitled The Pilgrimage of Man* (London: 1859). "F. D.," who writes the preface of the latter of these, regards the doctrine implied in this fourteenth-century allegory as distinctly "Protestant." The pilgrim's guide to the Heavenly City is Grace. Some of the other personifications are Industry, Idleness, Gluttony, Luxury, Sloth. Much is made of the Christian armor of Ephesians 6.

[4] John Brown, *John Bunyan (1628–1688), His Life, Times and Work,* the Tercentenary Edition, revised by Frank Mott Harrison (London: Hulburt Publishing Co., 1928), chap. xii.

explored with some care by Gerald R. Owst.[5] This writer
points out that Dent's *Plain Man's Pathway to Heaven*
(1601) (which came to Bunyan, as we have seen, with his
bride) contains allegorical figures that were stock material
of medieval sermon literature; and he holds that Bunyan's
imagination was kindled by memories of old books of homi-
lies. The closest parallel appears to be with a treatise discovered in manuscript by Dr. Owst, and reported in 1928,
entitled *Weye to Paradys*, written about 1400 and based
upon French sources. The work describes a pilgrim with a
sack, representing sin, upon his shoulders, who is obliged to
cross a watery abyss. A crude drawing illustrates his difficult
and perilous passage. Owst has also shown parallels in *The
Holy War* to the numerous medieval homiletic allegories of
the *castellum animae*, or "castle of the soul." The theme
could be attached to Scripture, for in Luke 10:38 the Vulgate
has "*Intravit Jesus in castellum*" ("Jesus entered the [forti-
fied] town").[6] William York Tindall finds Owst's suggestions unconvincing with respect to *The Holy War* but
probably sound as they apply to *Pilgrim's Progress*, and in
this connection points to evidence of the considerable extent
of Bunyan's unconfessed nonscriptural reading.[7] Some of this
he himself acknowledged. We have seen that he read, and
continued to prize, Luther's *Galations:* it was "next to the
Bible" among "all the books" he had seen. This language
implies acquaintance with a fair number of books. Some
range of reading in fiction and history is implied in the

[5] *Literature and Pulpit in Medieval England* (Cambridge: University Press, 1933), pp. 97–109.

[6] *Ibid.*, pp. 77 ff.

[7] *John Bunyan, Mechanick Preacher* (New York: Columbia University Press, 1934), pp. 145, 190 ff. Dr. Tindall's footnotes for his
chapters vii to ix (pp. 266–286) are valuable to those interested in
Bunyan's sources. For the seventeenth-century background an indispensable study is Helen C. White's *English Devotional Literature
(Prose) 1600–1640* (Madison: University of Wisconsin Press, 1931).

"Author's Preface" to *The Holy War*, especially in the lines beginning: "Of stories, well I know there's divers sorts." It is an obvious error, then, to suppose that Bunyan knew no literature except the Bible. Yet it was the Bible, studied, appropriated and remembered verse by verse, that mainly furnished his stock of ideas and prompted his literary activity. "Am I afraid," he asks in the "Author's Apology" to *Pilgrim's Progress*

> to say that holy writ
> Which for its style and phrase puts down all wit,
> Is everywhere so full of all these things,
> Dark figures, allegories? Yet there springs
> From that same book that lustre and those rays
> Of light that turn our darkest nights to days.

There was undoubtedly a psychopathic element in Bunyan's experience. His case is a favorite one for psychologists who study the phenomena of conversion. William James refers to the verbal automatisms, which consisted usually of Scripture texts, that kept recurring to his mind.[8] James and J. B. Pratt[9] are among the numerous psychologists who have observed similar diseased forms of preconversion anxiety in other Christian and non-Christian subjects. Bunyan himself observes the surprising and rapid fluctuations of anguish and delight occasioned by this battery of Scripture phrases upon his brain: once he speaks of it as the disturbed balance of "a pair of scales within my mind." At times in *Grace Abounding* the "pilgrim" appears to be making no "progress"— the sequence of moods appears wholly irrational; and in the end we are not made quite sure why permanent relief came when it did. Elements of the old disorder may have lingered

[8] *The Varieties of Religious Experience,* 28th impression (New York: Longmans, Green, 1917), pp. 157 ff.
[9] *The Religious Consciousness* (New York: Macmillan, 1920), chap. vii.

in the form of radical doubt. He was no stranger to the noisome dungeon of Doubting Castle. In the "Conclusion" of his narrative he writes:

Of all the temptations that ever I met in my life, to question the being of God and the truth of his gospel is the worst, and the worst to be borne. When this temptation comes, it takes my girdle from me, and removes the foundation from under me.

This experience undoubtedly helps to explain the ample charity with which Christian protects Little-Faith from Hopeful's condemnatory judgment. "No man can tell what in that combat attends us, but he that hath been in the battle himself. . . . But I trow, you will put some difference between Little-Faith and [Great-Grace] the King's champion. All the King's subjects are not his champions."

With a weaker nervous system, Bunyan might have ended his career in Bedlam. But he always held to some body of belief and never resigned himself to complete despair. Through the very tempests of his soul something permanently sustaining—a spiritual strength not otherwise available to him—became his in secure possession. Twelve years, ending at the age of forty-four, in a dirty, crowded prison might have made another sensitive and imaginative man quite unfit for social life. Instead, Bunyan resumed where he had left off. He at once became pastor of a church, preached well-constructed sermons and wrote bold and searching tracts. It was probably not until his second brief imprisonment—this time in the newly rebuilt town jail on the bridge over the Ouse—in 1675 that he "fell suddenly into an allegory."

Thus *The Pilgrim's Progress* was conceived and born. In the "Author's Apology" Bunyan presents, in shrewd rhymed prose, an admirable preface. He indicates that the book was "scribbled" with ease and delight in "vacant seasons." Evidently it was not based upon a carefully premeditated plot but was an unplanned natural accretion of imagined incidents in a "progress from this world to that which is to come." He wrote, he says, not to please others but to gratify himself. Yet he is aware that the story carries an effective message:

> This book will make a traveler of thee,
> If by its counsel thou wilt ruled be.

II

The "den" in which Bunyan says he slept and dreamed is, of course, his prison. He had long before learned, like his contemporary, Richard Lovelace, that "Stone walls do not a prison make" to the mind. And we should remember that, vile as the jail that housed him may have been, his was not the exhausting activity which many a war captive in our time has had to endure. It is true that healthy men loathe total inactivity. But a prisoner who is an integrated soul, and gifted with "the shaping spirit of imagination," though his body suffers from inactivity, is not to be too much pitied. Some well-traveled authors would probably have done better if they had been confined in a tidy modern prison. Even if we never enter the kind of den Bunyan knew, we are likely to have others and at the least to suffer enforced interruptions of our work and freedom of movement. Bunyan is a great example of the possibility of exploiting the spiritual opportunities of the "dens" into which we fall. In his case restraint of the body veritably enhances the liberty of the mind. He is amply compensated for a merely physical confinement by a fully emancipated imagination which creates actors and actions in profusion and makes the universe their arena.

Before we realize what is happening, the movement begins, like the smooth, accelerating motion of a great airliner as it leaves the runway. Presently the man with the burden and the book is disclosed walking in the fields. Variously misadvised by his neighbors in the City of Destruction, and crying, "What must I do to be saved?" he now "looked this way and that way, as if he would run." Soon after, he is directed on his way by Evangelist: "So I saw in my dream that the man began to run." Presently we find the people of Bunyan's creation in full tide of activity, running, contending, arguing, and, if we have not by now quite forgotten the prisoner and author, we become vividly aware of a great truth often rejected, that within narrow walls a man may be, by the gift of imagination, in the midst of a vast scene of urgent and excited action.

The City of Destruction, from which the awakened sinner puts forth, is, in a sense, our secular society. More closely observed it appears to be the community of sin, the company of those who live on the level of self-sufficient secularity. Plainly Bunyan sees it in a lost and hopeless state. While Christian prays for and pities his wife and children, who think him "distempered," he knows he must part from them and take flight from the city, leaving it to await the wrath to come. Bunyan's eschatology is marked by immediacy and realism: "Our city will be burnt with fire from heaven." Dr. Tindall has argued that in *The Holy War* he was voicing the apocalyptic notions of the Fifth Monarchy Men. This seems very probable. But here it is not necessary to suppose that he intends Christian to announce the imminent catastrophic end or complete transformation of human society. The crisis is really more of an individual matter. By nature death comes to every man: "I am condemned to die, and after that to come to judgment." For death and judgment the sinner is unprepared, and cannot be prepared until he has departed from the city of doomed secularity. Evangelist essays to show him the way on which he must go, but the new convert's vision is not clear. At this point, the art with which truth is embodied in the tale could hardly be surpassed. A learned sermon forty-five minutes in length would never say so much about faith and action as these few words:

Then said Evangelist, pointing with his finger over a very wide field, "Do you see yonder wicket gate?" The man said, "No." Then said the other, "Do you see yonder shining light?" He said, "I think I do." Then said Evangelist, "Keep that light in thine eyes, and go up directly thereto."

With this, the ragged, eager seeker of eternal life—his faith still measured by the phrase, "I think I do"—speeds on his way.

So fascinating are the opening paragraphs of the book that the reader is eager to know what may next befall the runner on his course. But in terms of religious interpretation the impression first created may be somewhat misleading. Salvation is an individual matter, but it is later seen to be highly social and ethical in its outworkings. It is not merely a flight but a communion. Christian will have warm companionship on the way, and he has not, we shall find, parted with his family forever. Moreover, Bunyan deserves to be read at large, not only in his greatest work. There are passages in *The Holy War* and in the tract on *Christian Behavior* in which he shows a deep concern for temporal affairs and social duty. Mansoul is not only the life of the individual but, in Bunyan's phrase, "the metropolis of the world." By Christian's flight Bunyan does not mean that in order to take the way of salvation we must abandon all mundane obligations and connections. In this respect he is more healthily positive than many of the sectarians of his time. But he would have us seek first the Kingdom of God, and seek it with singlehearted devotion.

III

The Pilgrim's way is not often lonely: there is great traffic of characters good and bad. Those who would hinder and mislead Christian are the earthbound lovers of things seen and temporal, such as Obstinate, Worldly Wiseman and the flighty pretenders to piety—Pliable, Talkative and By-ends. It is Bunyan's habit to allow such characters eloquent if brief utterance of their opinions and then to consign them to their fate. To seek "an inheritance incorruptible" is in Obstinate's judgment the mark of "a crazy-headed coxcomb." With solid conviction he goes back to the doomed city. Bunyan, like other preachers, had met many an Obstinate, and he has no effective persuasion for him. Pliable has inconsiderately decided to join the pilgrimage. Since he bears no burden of conviction of sin, he finds burdened Christian's pace too slow for him, and trips lightly by his side until both fall into the Slough of Despond and are "bedaubed with dirt." Then Pliable, reproaching his companion, leaves him to labor through the mire and seek the heavenly country alone, while he himself scrambles out where he fell in and ingloriously scurries to his house. Pliable's reasoning is: "If we have such ill speed at our first setting out, what may we expect betwixt this and our journey's end?" The dreamer is permitted to see poor Pliable back at home, where he sits "sneaking" among his old neighbors; and later, Faithful reports to Christian that the recreant is held in derision by all sorts of people and is seven times worse than if he had never started out.

Mr. Worldly Wiseman of the town of Carnal Policy seeks to persuade Christian to abandon the strenuous journey and directs him to the village of Morality ("where," says Bunyan shrewdly, "there are houses now standing empty") promising that there Mr. Legality will readily relieve him of

BUNYAN: *Pilgrim's Progress*   103

the burden under which he groans. But presently fires flash
from the hill that towers over the village; these are the
lightnings of Sinai, the terrors of the law. The Pilgrim
quakes for fear, and lo, Evangelist, whose counsel he has
disobeyed, draws near to rescue and rebuke him.

It is at a later stage, while Christian and Faithful are ex-
changing experiences, that Talkative, "a tall man," steps up
beside them and begins to exhibit his nimble mastery of the
clichés of evangelical religion. In fact he will be delighted
to talk of anything: of things heavenly or earthly, moral or
evangelical, sacred or profane, past or future, foreign or
domestic, essential or circumstantial. Shakespeare's Nick
Bottom is not more accommodating. "Now did Faithful begin to wonder"; and Christian reveals that their new companion is one whose religion is to make a noise with his
tongue, and who is a churl to his servants and harder to deal
with than a Turk. Good men are ashamed of him and blush
when his name is mentioned. Bunyan's age produced many
of Talkative's kind: men who, as Faithful here remarks, "cry
out against sin in the pulpit, yet can abide it well enough in
the heart, house and conversation." Of all such, Talkative
remains a horrible example.

The character of Mr. By-ends is even more brilliantly and
satirically drawn. Christian, after numerous adventures, is in
the company of Hopeful when Mr. By-ends of the town of
Fairspeech offers the travelers his cheerful company. He explains that he and his wife, who is Lady Feigning's daughter,

differ in religion from those of the stricter sort: yet in but two
small points. First, we never strive against wind and tide. Secondly, we are always most zealous when religion goes in his
silver slippers; we love much to walk with him in the street, if
the sun shines and the people applaud him.

Christian will not have his companionship on these terms.
"You must go against wind and tide . . . You must own

Religion in rags." To this uncompromising answer By-ends enters the plea of toleration: "You must not . . . lord it over my faith; leave me to my liberty, and let me go with you." "Not a step further," says Christian. By-ends will never desert his principles: he will join other companions. Here the austere puritan parts company with the latitudinarian. Dr. Tindall argues very effectively that By-ends in real life was the Reverend Edward Fowler, later Bishop of Gloucester, author of *The Design of Christianity* (1671) and other treatises. Fowler was an advocate of that compliance which he himself practiced when at the Restoration he was transformed from a Presbyterian into an Episcopalian.[10] Bunyan assailed Fowler in a tract of 1672, and here he gives no quarter to the position of Fowler's image, By-ends; of whom, indeed, we should expect some flexibility since he is the cordial admirer of his fellow townsmen, my Lord Turnabout and Mr. Facing-both-ways, and of his uncle, Parson Two-Tongues. The "principles" to which By-ends adheres appear to be those of a moral coward who has rationalized his cowardice. Presently, he is enjoying the bad company of Hold-the-World, Money-love and Save-all, and he soon falls into the silver mine of Demas and is never seen again on the way. In Part II of *The Pilgrim's Progress* Greatheart recalls By-ends as "a downright hypocrite" who "had his mode of religion for every fresh occasion."

These and similar figures represent the hindrances and temptations that in real life the Christian must encounter, whether in human guise or in the promptings of the heart. Not less vividly portrayed are the good counselors and befriending spirits that attend the traveler. When Christian, deserted by Pliable, has struggled to the farther edge of the Slough of Despond, "a man whose name was Help" lifts him by the hand and sets him on firm ground. We need not

---

[10] W. Y. Tindall, *op. cit.*, chap. iii.

elaborate theologically the role of the man whose name was Help. In life's vicissitudes, ofttimes by human agency, he brings his measureless comfort to the spent soul. Perhaps Bunyan had read in Thomas Norton's translation of Calvin's *Institutes* (I, v, 8): "how God in cases past hope, doeth sodenly and wonderfully and beside all hope succor men that are in miserie and in a manner lost." But he simply cites Psalm 40:2: "He brought me out of an horrible pit."

The Pilgrim's timely adviser in moments of peril is Evangelist. Bunyan has him enter from time to time like an Olympian deity in the *Aeneid* to exhort and direct the wayfarer. His advice, however, identifies him as the Christian minister and guide of souls, and doubtless his importance in the allegory is given him by the author's experience of the helpful advice of good John Gifford of Bedford. Where necessary he can be a stern monitor. When Worldly Wiseman has led Christian from the way and directed him to the fire-flashing hill by Legality's house, it is time for Evangelist to redirect the wanderer's steps. With unconscious art, Bunyan dramatizes his entrance. He "drew nearer and nearer . . . with a severe and dreadful countenance." Christian trembles before him, and under his rebuke begins "to cry out lamentably." The Gospel itself is stern toward those who lapse into prudential morality. But it welcomes their repentance. As Christian departs with anxious haste to return to the way, Evangelist dismisses him with a kiss, a smile and Godspeed. Later, when Christian, with his new companion Faithful, is approaching Vanity Fair, Evangelist holds gracious discourse with them and in kindness warns them of the temptations and sufferings soon to be encountered.

Midway on his journey, Christian finds a stalwart companion in Faithful, who has also begun at the prompting of Evangelist but has come by a different way. The breadth of Bunyan's conception of Christianity is apparent in his wholly admiring treatment of Faithful, whose religious experience is of a different pattern from his own. Faithful has had no exhausting agonies of conversion. Arthur Porter has remarked that he is "not one of the twice-born."[11] However, he has felt from the first the condemnation of the Law, and on the way he learns the mercy of the Gospel. Bunyan takes (and gives) delight in the incident of Christian's overtaking Faithful on the way. Looking forward from an "ascent" that has been cast up for the purpose of giving pilgrims a forward view of the road, he spies Faithful plodding ahead, and calls aloud: "Ho, ho; so-ho; stay and I will be your companion." Faithful cannot delay, so Christian with an effort runs by him, casting toward him a vainglorious smile, only to fall and be helped to his feet again by Faithful. "Then I saw in my dream, they went lovingly on together and had sweet discourse."

Both moral faithfulness and religious faith are manifest in the character of Faithful. He explains that he had left the City of Destruction after Christian's departure and had reached the Wicket-gate without passing through the Slough of Despond. One whose name was Wanton had sought to allure him, and he had shut his eyes that he might not be bewitched by her. Then, at the foot of the Hill Difficulty, a very aged man named Adam the First had invited him to his house of many delights. When he departed from Old Adam, Faithful relates, "he gave me such a deadly twitch back that I thought he had pulled part of me after himself." For his hesitation here, he felt the penalty of the Law. He tells how Moses, a man swift as the wind, pursued him and was beating him to death, when One with pierced hands "came by and bid him forbear." He had also encountered

[11] *The Inside of Bunyan's Dream* (New York: Fleming H. Revell, 1927), p. 180.

Discontent, and had been hard pressed by Shame, who said that religion was "a pitiful, low, sneaking business" and proved himself a bold and persistent villain.

The man of immovable faith enjoys immunity from what is represented by the Slough of Despond and by the lions in the path to the House Beautiful. The lions had been sleeping when Faithful passed by at noon, and he had not paused to enter the palace. Thus, not halting for fear or for consolation, he moves on to a glorious close. Faithful, it turns out, is appointed to die a martyr death in Vanity Fair, condemned by Lord Hate-good and a jury of rogues under the laws of Pharaoh and Nebuchadnezzar; but "a chariot and a couple of horses" wait for him and he is "carried up through the clouds with sound of trumpet, the nearest way to the celestial gate."

These, together with Christian himself, are the leading persons of the drama in Part I. Each of them remains an unforgettable figure in the reader's memory. Almost equally rich in characters, especially those on the side of the angels, is Part II. There two gracious women have constant prominence, Christiana, who announces herself "the wife of that pilgrim that some years ago did travel this way," and her solicitous and tender hearted young companion, Mercy. The two may owe something respectively to the second and the first Mrs. Bunyan. Like Shakespeare, Bunyan had a deep appreciation of womankind; even his satire of the sex is on the gentle side. Christiana's four boys are characters in a family comedy with grave undertones and are made to illustrate good religious training in the home. But Part II is not a book for women only. It is a book of combat, a book of courage, comfort and hard-earned joy. Its hero is Greatheart, the resourceful counselor and knightly protector of the gentle ladies, the slayer of giants and a man mighty in prayer. In their several masculine roles Sagacity, Honest, Steadfast and

Valiant-for-Truth likewise earn our admiration. Some memorable characters of both sexes appear also in the opposition party, such as Mrs. Timorous, who endeavors to dissuade Christiana from setting out on pilgrimage; Mr. Fearing, a lugubrious saint, who hesitates long on the brink of the Slough of Despond and thereafter carries "a Slough of Despond in his mind"; and the Man with the Muckrake who "can look no way but down."

The resourcefulness of Bunyan's genius is seen in the astonishing variety of the characters he has drawn. He can make scores of good folk admirable without making them alike, and without making them dull. The "woman whose name was Dull" belongs, as do Ignorance and Want-Wit, with the enemy. Similarly he can make the bad despicable in manifold ways and with diverting variations. Withal there is no confusion of good and bad, and badness itself is not diverting.

Allegory has not always been successfully handled in literature, and there is a stuffiness about many great allegories, such as *The Faery Queene,* that is wholly absent from *The Pilgrim's Progress.* It was probably of advantage to Bunyan that he wrote for a generation that had read John Earle's *Microcosmographie* (first published in the year of Bunyan's birth) and many other collections of character sketches. His own keen observation of persons may have been stimulated by an acquaintance with some of this character literature. Certainly his characters are almost never mere abstractions. Where other allegorists would be content with personifications trailing clouds of abstraction with them, Bunyan's personifications are at once clarified as persons. Great-Grace has the scars of many a battle on his face. Christiana forgets her bottle of spirits and has to send her little boy back to fetch it. Honest discerns in Feeble-Mind's "whitely look," the cast in his eye and his manner of speech a family resemblance

to Fearing. He furnishes, too, a Chaucerian description of
Madame Bubble, the very spirit of worldly vanity, a tall,
comely dame with a great purse by her side who "speaks
very smoothly and gives you a smile at the end of a sentence."

And what reader of Bunyan can forget the highly indi-
vidualized demonic monsters and giants who here and there
appear. Someone perusing this page may share with me a
recollection of the classroom of Professor Paul T. Lafleur
of McGill University, as he recited: "Then Apollyon strad-
dled quite over the whole breadth of the way," and added
(with index finger gravely laid along the line of his noble
nose and then thrust forward with cumulative emphasis):
"Gentlemen, when you can write like that you will not need
to attend my classes!" He was, I think, too wise to expect
that any of us would write like that. But Bunyan does it
effortlessly. With startling brevity of phrase he flashes these
clear and arresting pictures, fresh from their creation, upon
the reader's mind. When Giant Despair, walking early, dis-
covers Christian and Hopeful asleep on his grounds, "with a
grim and surly voice he bid them awake." Atheist, hearing
Christian say that he was going to Mount Zion, "fell into a
great laughter." Greatheart, champion of the helpless in their
need, comes in the nick of time to the haunt of Slay-Good,
to find that flesh-eating giant "with one Mr. Feeble-Mind
in his hand . . . with purpose to pick his bones." This is the
kind of writing that cannot be taught.

IV

Christian himself fascinates us more by his experiences
than by his qualities. Yet in one respect he is the greatest
of Bunyan's characters, since he stands for any Christian,

and combines the faith and fears, wisdom and error, virtues
and faults of the common run of saints-in-training. He is no
faultless Grandison or Galahad. He is one who, with limited
strength, must battle frightful forms of evil and withstand
subtle temptations; one who may be beguiled into misadven-
ture and suffer spiritual reverses even as you and I, but who
has the root of the matter in him and triumphs by good intention and the grace of God.

There is a terrific urgency about Christian's departure
from the City of Destruction. "So I saw in my dream that
the man began to run." That he might not hear the protests
of his wife and children, "the man put his fingers on his ears
and ran on crying, 'Life, life, eternal life!'" We have seen
how the heroic zeal of the convert, symbolized in this speed
and resolution, is relaxed in the incident with Worldly
Wiseman, who proposes an easy way of pretended deliverance. Under Evangelist's severe rebuke, Christian repents of
this, returns to the way and "in process of time" reaches
the Wicket-gate, and pleads before it:

> Will he within
> Open to sorry me, though I have been
> An undeserving rebel?

Goodwill opens the door and quickly pulls him within
lest the arrows shot from Beelzebub's near-by castle should
strike the suppliant. The Wicket-gate gives entrance to the
straight and narrow way. Bunyan gives us no hint that he
identifies it with believer's baptism, but it is an initiation
into the fellowship of the companions of the way. A Christian's life cannot be all motion without contemplation; and
soon the Pilgrim is in the House of the Interpreter where he
is shown by symbols various aspects of religious truth. It is

the Holy Spirit who is instructing the soul. The picture he first sees, of a very grave person with the best of books in his hand and the world behind his back, is drawn doubtless with a memory of John Gifford and represents a preacher of the Gospel, authorized guide of the religious traveler.

The superiority of the Gospel over the Law is aptly expressed in a parable of the dust-filled parlor swept and cleaned. The contrast of the two little lads, Passion and Patience, sitting in their chairs, affords a lesson for those tempted to take the cash and let the credit go. One of Bunyan's best mottoes for the Puritan's wall is set here: "Patience is willing to wait." There are of course some matters of urgency for which we may not wait. The reader will remember this passage by contrast when in Part II he sees Mercy urgently knocking at the Wicket-gate: "Now Mercy began to be very impatient, and each minute was as long to her as an hour." Here, too, is the "Man in the Iron Cage." He is the incarnation of despair, and Bunyan knows him well. He has had a lurid dream of judgment, in describing which he says: "The bottomless pit opened just whereabout I stood."

Christian takes the road again. It is fenced by the walls of salvation and it leads up to a cross. These pictures reproduce the English landscapes Bunyan knew: a cross stood in Elstow village. Bunyan adds a sepulcher below the cross. Now occurs the miracle of deliverance. The Pilgrim has labored until now under his burden of conviction of sin. At the cross the burden is loosed from off his shoulders, tumbles into the sepulcher and is seen no more. While he weeps with gratitude and wonder, he is greeted by three Shining Ones, the first of whom says: "Thy sins be forgiven thee"; the second replaces his rags with fair raiment; and the third sets a mark on his forehead and gives him a sealed roll, which is a certificate to be presented at the celestial gate and, as we later learn, to be read for comfort on the way. "Then Christian gave three leaps for joy, and went on singing.   ."

The insincerity of church members, rather than avowed opposition to Christianity, is exemplified by many of those whom Christian encounters. Such are the three fettered sleepers, Simple, Sloth and Presumption, who perish because they refuse to bestir themselves, and that most un-Puritanic pair, Formalist and Hypocrisy, who have entered the way irregularly by scaling the wall. Refreshing himself at the spring at the foot of the Hill Difficulty, Christian starts its hard ascent, while Formalist avoids it by entering the path called Danger, and Hypocrisy by the way of Destruction, where among dark mountains "he fell, and rose no more." The steepness of the hill forces Christian from running to walking, then to his hands and knees. Halfway to the top is an Arbor, which, like the spring, is for spiritual refreshment; but when Christian uses it as a place of sleep he must be aroused and sent on his way. During sleep, alas, the roll has fallen from his hand. When at the top Mistrust and Timorous have warned him of lions in the way, he misses the roll —the assurance of his acceptance at the desired haven—and in deep contrition he goes back for it. "How many steps," says Christian, "have I taken in vain."

Lions menace the approach to the House Beautiful. It is better not to interpret them too exactly. Every individual knows where they lurk and roar. The note that "the lions were chained but he saw not their chains" is Bunyan's pictorial way of saying: "We have nothing to fear but fear itself." Watchful, the porter, explains that they are placed there "for trial of faith." At his direction Christian goes through to the portal, and after questioning is admitted to the palace by "a grave and beautiful damsel named Discretion."

Three other maidens, Piety, Prudence and Charity, are appointed to discourse with Christian at the supper, and their questions are designed to draw forth reflections upon his experiences. He admits that sinful impulses persist in him, but he has his "golden hours" of victory. "The name of the chamber was Peace, where he slept till break of day." In the morning he is instructed in the "rarities" and ancient records of the place—a lesson in church history—and he visits the armory and views famous relics such as Moses' rod, Jael's hammer and nail and the jawbone wielded by Samson. From the House Beautiful he is shown also the Delectable Mountains in Immanuel's Land. But this inviting region lies beyond the Valley of Humiliation, a battle ground of the soul. Hence it is appropriate that the Pilgrim should be taken to the armory again before his departure and "harnessed from head to foot" but, since he may not retreat, with no armor for his back.

Thus accoutered in stanch armor he enters the valley and is confronted by the foul fiend and scaly monster, Apollyon, who has the mouth of a lion and views the traveler's approach "with a disdainful countenance." Before the battle, there is an exchange of accusations, in which the fiend truthfully charges Christian with faults already known to us. "All this is true," says the Pilgrim, "and much more which thou hast left out, but the Prince whom I serve and honor is merciful and ready to forgive." Enraged, the demon bestrides the road and flings a flaming dart, which is parried by Christian's shield. The dire combat that ensues lasts more than half a day and is vividly related in three hundred words.

Christian, having lost his sword, recovers it and, quoting appropriate Scriptures, inflicts a deadly wound. "With that Apollyon spread forth his dragon wings and sped him away, that Christian saw him no more."

It is perhaps noteworthy that although Christian now gives thanks for divine deliverance, no visible heavenly champion has been sent to his aid. The man who is equipped with the shield of faith, the sword of the Spirit and a memory of helpful Bible verses is more than a match for the Devil. He soon receives from a supernatural hand leaves of the tree of life to heal his wounds, and he refreshes himself from the bottle of wine which was a parting gift from the virgins of the House Beautiful. The Church has blessings for the soul spent and wounded in combat with demonic evil.

But the way leads now into an extension of the Valley of Humiliation—the Valley of the Shadow of Death. Affrighted men, like the spies who brought an evil report of Canaan, warn Christian back; but he advances with drawn sword along a dark path between a deep ditch and a quagmire. Hard by the wayside is the flaming mouth of hell, and as he passes it a fiend whispers blasphemies in his ears. The region of demons, hobgoblins and dragons gives place to one of snares and pitfalls, which would have been fatal, but "just then the sun was rising."

In a cave at the end of this Valley of the Shadow Christian finds two giants, Pope and Pagan, of whom the latter has been long dead and the former, "stiff in his joints," sits biting his nails and says to the passing wayfarer, "You will never mend till more of you be burned." This brief fragment of satire seems like a reproduction of the materials of some seventeenth-century caricature, and like a caricature it oversimplifies and exaggerates its message.

V

The companionship of Christian and Faithful, and their interview with Talkative, have already been noticed. The exhortation of Evangelist, in which Vanity Fair is described, and the narrative of the trial scene at the fair constitute a notable feature of the book. If *The Labyrinth of the World*, written in Czech by John Amos Comenius in 1623 and published in 1631, had been available to Bunyan, we would suspect an indebtedness; but this book was rendered into English only in our own century. When Comenius' pilgrim examines the governing class, the rich and the pleasure lovers, notable resemblances to Bunyan's Vanity Fair appear. Comenius has a law court in which the chief justice, Lord Icommandit, is assisted by Atheist, Person-respecter, Lovegold and other judges; Gossip, Lie and Suspicion are witnesses; Flatterer and Prattler are attorneys. Bunyan's characters in the trial of Faithful are an even more reprehensible lot. In their creation some of the author's resentment against the courts that had condemned him finds vent. The scene is manifestly Charles II's England, and Bunyan dares to call the Lord of the Fair Beelzebub. Lord Hate-good, who presides, resembles Judge Jeffreys. The jurors, who bear such names as Blindman, Live-loose, Liar, Cruelty and Implacable, are incarnations of sins which Bunyan undoubtedly felt to be characteristic of the Restoration ruling class. The friends of Beelzebub, whom Faithful has railed at, include the aristocratic rakes, Lord Carnal Delight and old Lord Lechery, and that rapacious knight, Sir Having Greedy. The witnesses, Envy, Superstition and Pickthank, are also of the time: Faithful's answer to Superstition states the stock Puritan claims against the established Church. The cruelty of the cage and the pillory, the mockeries and tortures suffered by

Christian and his companion, reflect memories of Noncon-
formist experience in the 1670's. But all this has a wider
and nonecclesiastical reference. The association of voluptu-
ousness and cruelty is not confined to one era or to one nation. Comenius had observed it in central Europe. His pilgrim, visiting the haunts of pleasure, remarks: "These halls
certainly are more cheerful than the torture-chambers un-
derneath."[12]

Christian, by the help of God, escapes the prison he has
shared with Faithful. As he sets off again, he sings a song in
praise of his departed companion, which ends:

> For though they killed thee, thou art yet alive.

The heroic martyrdom of Faithful may possibly be intended to recall the end of the era of Cromwellian Puritanism. In that case the survival and perpetuation of Puritan
ideals will be recognized in Hopeful, who under the impulse
of Faithful's testimony now attaches himself to Christian.
But, of itself, any such special application of the allegory is
inadequate. When in Doubting Castle Hopeful presents the
arguments against suicide and when in the River of Death he
reassures his frightened companion: "Be of good cheer, . . .
I feel the bottom and it is good," we see more clearly the
significance of his name. We are saved by hope.

The discussion with By-ends, noted above, leads to an
argument with his associates, in course of which Money-love
offers a labored justification of a minister who for gain or
advantage alters his principles. Christian here becomes a
preacher, and in a sermon under five heads concludes that
the view of Money-love is heathenish, hypocritical and

---

[12] John Amos Comenius, *The Labyrinth of the World and the
Paradise of the Heart*, translated by Mathew Spinka (Chicago: National Union of Czechoslovak Protestants in America, 1942), chaps.
xix, xxiv, xxv.

devilish. The preacher is so impressive that at the end his hearers stand mutely "staring one upon another." Christian cautiously restrains Hopeful from obeying the call of Demas, "Ho, turn aside hither," an invitation to destruction in the depths of the silver mine beside the Hill Lucre where By-ends perishes. But beside the pleasant River of Life Christian misleads Hopeful into By-path Meadow, where they follow one Vain-Confidence. When their guide falls into a pit, it is Hopeful who, since Christian's mind is troubled by his error, leads the way back, through dangerous floods that meanwhile have arisen. They escape drowning but find themselves on the estate of Giant Despair and are presently lodged in a dark dungeon of Doubting Castle, deprived of food, drink and light. The giant's wife, Diffidence, counsels him night after night to take measures that will insure their destruction—their passing from doubt to despair. But despite the blows of his crab-tree cudgel, the suggestions of suicide and frightful threatenings, they retain a spark of life. Christian falls into a swoon, but comes to himself again, and Hopeful recalls to his mind that he has been "valiant heretofore." They endure this treatment from Wednesday morning until midnight Saturday, when they turn to prayer. At daybreak Christian bethinks himself that he has in his bosom the key Promise; with it they escape through an inner and an outer door, though the lock of the latter "went damnably hard." (In some texts, editorial censors have changed "damnably" to "desperately.")

Having reached the Delectable Mountains, the pilgrims are refreshed, washed and nourished. Guided by the Shepherds, Knowledge, Experience, Watchful and Sincere, they traverse the mountains of Error and Caution and view dimly through a "perspective glass" the gates of the Celestial City. With the farewell of the Shepherds, the dreamer awakes. The author seems to have been interrupted at this point, possibly by the events connected with his liberation from prison. But the text resumes: "And I slept and dreamed again."

Christian narrates the story of Little-Faith who, at this stage of the journey, lost his spending money and narrowly escaped death at the hands of three sturdy highwaymen, Faintheart, Mistrust and Guilt. The King's champion, Great-Grace, puts the rogues to flight. Christian makes much of the point that Little-Faith has kept his jewels and his certificate of admittance to the Celestial City; he would arrive, though he would have to beg his way and suffer "many a hungry belly." They that have saving faith, however weak, cannot yield or sell their salvation.

The encounters with Flatterer, who catches the wayfarers in his net, and with Atheist, who after long search has concluded that the Celestial City does not exist, are instructively narrated. Christian and Hopeful now reach the Enchanted Ground, whose air makes travelers drowsy. To keep themselves awake they engage in a discussion of religious experience, which will hardly keep awake the reader who has the livelier *Grace Abounding* in his mind. Yet there are here some fresh and penetrating judgments and pertinent analogies. We cannot settle an old debt to the shopkeeper merely by paying for current purchases; and on the other hand, our daily offenses would damn us even if our previous record were faultless. Hence the necessity of atonement, and of repentance.

Ignorance, a brisk, self-confident and insolent "youngster," encountered earlier, joins the pilgrims in the Enchanted Ground, but after long dialogue, being without faith, he cannot keep pace with them and comes "hobbling after." We are informed that "it will go ill with him at last." Nor does Bunyan leave us in any doubt about the final fate of Ignorance. Aided by Vain-hope, a ferryman, he passes the

River of Death with ease, only to be turned away from the
Celestial Gate and carried through a door in the side of the
hill. It is an epitaph, startling and pathetic, upon poor, mis-
guided Ignorance that Bunyan writes at the end of the book:

Then I saw that there was a way to hell even from the gate
of heaven, as well as from the City of Destruction.

VI

Entering the country of Beulah, the pilgrims find themselves out of sight of Doubting Castle and within sight of
the Heavenly City. Beholding its fair structures gleaming in
sunlight, Christian becomes sick with desire for that glorious
home. This nostalgia for Jerusalem the Golden is a familiar
feature of the literature of piety. In that long poem, first
published by the Lutheran controversialist Matthew Flacius,
to which Archbishop Trench gave the title *Laus Patriae
Caelestis* (*Praise of the Heavenly Country*), Bernard of
Cluny has a section beginning "*Urbs Syon aurea*," some lines
of which read, in the familiar translation of J. M. Neale:

> They stand, those halls of Zion,
>   Conjubilant with song,
> And bright with many an angel,
>   And all the martyr throng.

Bunyan cannot have known Bernard's *Praise of the Heav-
eanly Country*, but his is essentially the same heaven, and it
is presented with the same fascination and fresh astonishment.

In Bunyan's boyhood this longing for heaven lighted
many a passage in the spiritual letters of Samuel Rutherford;
during his young manhood it was memorably treated by
Richard Baxter in *The Saints' Everlasting Rest*. "O for the
long day, and the high sun, and the fair garden and the
King's great City up above these visible heavens," exclaims
the Scottish mystic, and again: "Faint not, the miles to

heaven are few and short." "There," writes Baxter, "is the glorious new Jerusalem, the gates of pearl, . . . streets and pavements of transparent gold." Bunyan often dwells upon these pictures and emotions; but here he has expressed them in words simple and quaint with a depth of yearning and a glow of anticipation hardly surpassed.

It was builded of pearls and precious stones, also the streets thereof were paved with gold; so that by reason of the natural glory of the city, and the reflection of the sunbeams upon it, Christian with desire fell sick; Hopeful also had a fit or two of the same disease; wherefore here they lay by it awhile, crying out because of their pangs, "If you see my Beloved, tell him that I am sick of love."

They enter now fair orchards, vineyards and gardens, and approach the gate of the city. But the River of Death still separates the pilgrims from their eternal home. All the fear of death was experienced in the Valley of the Shadow; but this is the thing itself. The pilgrims would fain have escaped the deep waters, but that is denied them. They are informed, however, that they will find it deeper or shallower as they believe in the King of the place. Christian is soon beyond his depth; "Hopeful had much ado to keep his brother's head above water." Bunyan does not make death easy, nor does he sentimentalize it, for those heavenward bound.

We may ask why it is that Christian must receive comfort from another in the same agony. Men do not ordinarily die together, but alone. Incidents like the last scenes of the Scott expedition, or the last brotherly stand of the remnants of a doomed battalion, are unusual, and we should expect Bunyan to deal with what is typical. There is a word of Luther's, written in 1520, that seems to have meaning here. Luther is explaining the nature of the Communion of Saints. "Christ," he says, "has not willed that the way of death, from which every man shrinks, should be solitary for us, but we go the way of suffering and death with the whole Church as our comrade [*comite tota ecclesia*]." Something of this notion is needed to explain Hopeful's role at the deep river. Every saint of the Church is saying to the Christian at his departing: "Be of good cheer, my brother. I feel the bottom and it is good."

The Bedford Tinker does not vulgarize his eschatology. Gladness and sublimity could hardly be more effectively combined. "O, by what tongue or pen can their glorious joy be expressed!" Bunyan exclaims, even while he is expressing it so well that we hear the melodies and see the angels. The pilgrims are transfigured as they enter the gate; and the once sinful bell ringer of Elstow adds: "Then I heard in my dream that all the bells in the city rang for joy."

WILLIAM LAW

A Serious Call to a Devout and Holy
Life

Chapter V

WILLIAM LAW:

A Serious Call to a Devout and Holy Life

THE life span of William Law (1686–1761) embraces that of Joseph Butler, philosopher and churchman. In 1751 Bishop Butler, in addressing his clergy, remarked:

> For as different ages have been distinguished by different sorts of particular errors and vices, the deplorable distinction of ours is an avowed scorn of religion on the part of some and a growing disregard for it in the generality.[1]

When this judgment was uttered, John Wesley had already been thirteen years on journey. Butler, with his anxious fear of enthusiasm, was hardly in a position to appreciate what was astir among "the generality." But in 1751 it was too early to say that the tide was turning. New inventions were bringing on the industrial revolution, and the shifts of population consequent upon it would intensify some of the evils. Certainly, if it is taken as a judgment of conditions in England during the first half of the eighteenth century, Butler's sentence finds full support in modern research. Each of us has, perhaps, read various colorful descriptions of the coarseness, cruelty, drunkenness and debauchery, the scoffing at every expression of serious religion, the eloquence in profanity of the privileged classes, the

[1] *Works of Bishop Butler* (Oxford, 1850), II, 309.

dispirited squalor and neglected ignorance of the poor prevalent in that age of defection from vital Christianity. From 1720 to 1740 Walpole held sway. This was a period of new prosperity but of the greatest moral darkness in the history of England. A talented statesman of the lowest political morality, Walpole scorned all idealistic motives, placed a premium on venality and poisoned public life. It was in the Walpole era, the very nadir of religion and morality, that William Law challenged the dominant trend of the time in two related books, *A Practical Treatise Upon Christian Perfection* (1726) and *A Serious Call to a Devout and Holy Life* (1728).

William Law was the son of a grocer of King's Cliffe, Northamptonshire, where he was born February 3, 1686. He studied at Cambridge, becoming a fellow of Emmanuel College in 1711, took deacon's orders and apparently was for two years curate at Hastingfield. With the accession of George I, Law could not conscientiously abjure allegiance to the Stuarts. He abandoned his opening career in the Church of England and joined the Nonjurors. A great deepening of his religious life, by some referred to as conversion, occurred in 1720. Recent studies have shown that it was probably in 1723 that he became tutor to the household of Edward Gibbon at Putney. Mr. Gibbon's grandson, Edward Gibbon the historian, refers to Law as "the much honored friend and spiritual director of the whole family."[2] In 1727 he was ordained to the priesthood by a nonjuring bishop. He became the friend and spiritual adviser of a number of men of distinction, including the poet John Byrom and the versatile Scottish physician George Cheyne. John Wesley visited him for guidance first in July, 1732, and both he and

[2] *Autobiography of Edward Gibbon* (World Classics edition, 1907), p. 17.

his brother Charles consulted him at various times thereafter.[3] In 1740 Law took up his residence at King's Cliffe in a house inherited from his father.[4] Here he provided a home for Miss Hester Gibbon, devout aunt of the historian, and for the widow of a deceased friend, Archibald Hutcheson, M.P. The household was conducted on a strict religious plan, somewhat resembling that of Nicholas Ferrar's community of Little Gidding a century earlier. Law enjoyed good health to old age. He died, aged seventy-five, April 9, 1761.

As a man, he is not easily classified or compared with others. An ascetic bachelor, but ruddy and inclined to plumpness, he was in early life inclined to be opinionated, but he gave to most of those who knew him an impression of geniality and warmth. John Wesley once accused him of having become "morose," but the circumstances may have led Wesley so to interpret an attitude merely reticent and a little evasive. The discipline which he imposed upon himself was austere but not excessively rigorous. If he had lived in the Middle Ages he might have founded a monastery. But in typical monasticism his concern for the religious life of women and the education of girls would not have had an adequate outlet. He founded and maintained a school for girls at King's Cliffe. While he is very respectful to early monasticism, and even proposes its revival, he also insists on the religious opportunities and duties of those engaged in ordinary callings. Christian perfection, he says emphatically,

[3] On the relations of Law and Wesley, J. B. Green's careful study, *John Wesley and William Law* (London: Epworth, 1945), can be recommended. See on this point chap. iii.

[4] "G. Moreton," *Memorials of William Law* (London: 1895), gives a description with illustrations of the Hall Yard House which was Law's home. "Moreton" was in reality George Blacker Morgan; he used the pseudonym also as editor of Law's *Works*.

"calls no one to a cloister"; in the final chapter of the *Serious Call* this is modified to read: "calls no one (necessarily) to a cloister."

Law's ministry, unlike Wesley's, was almost exclusively to people of the higher social and economic strata. His life involved exacting routines rather than great struggles and expenditures of effort. The fact that his conscience denied him an ecclesiastical career under the Hanoverians was fortunate for his cultivation of piety. It afforded him a condition of detachment and literary ease denied to most. It would be highly ungracious and ungrateful on our part to begrudge these opportunities to the author of a religious classic.

II

William Law's title to our grateful remembrance lies not in what he did but in what he wrote. Of his series of substantial books and tracts, the best known is *A Serious Call to a Devout and Holy Life*. What characterized most of his writings, including this one, is that he courageously and cogently assailed the degraded standards and corrosive forces of his day and vigorously affirmed the exacting demands and incomparable values of Christianity. Mingling witty satire with urgent exhortation, he bade defiance to worldliness, ridiculed its devotees and invited his readers to the paths of holiness. With an intensity hardly surpassed by St. Bernard or Wesley, he asserted the claims of "religion in earnest" in opposition no less to the insincerities of a merely nominal churchmanship than to the frank desertion of religion and morality.

Apart from his early participation in ecclesiastical controversies, his writings fall into two fairly distinct periods. About 1733 he was led, through a work by a French Prot-

estant, Pierre Poiret, to enter upon the study of the works of
Jacob Böhme. Böhme transformed Law into a mystic. His
subsequent writings reflect an increasing familiarity with,
and acceptance of, mystical ideas. The Quaker scholar, Stephen Hobhouse, has given us a useful selection of these materials and presented therewith helpful notes of Law's
sources.[5] It may be necessary to point out that much of the
most sincere Christian piety is essentially nonmystical. There
are passages in Law's writings before 1733 that are in accord
with mystical religion, but as a whole they represent a piety
that is Biblical in inspiration and not more mystical than the
New Testament. They share this quality with the writings
of Bunyan, Baxter and Jeremy Taylor, popular seventeenth-
century English guides to the devout life. To Taylor, Law
was doubtless considerably indebted in the period in which
he wrote the *Serious Call,* but the book does not, I think, exhibit the indebtedness in traceable ways. It probably reflects
impressions from a wide range of reading, classical and
Christian; but to display the evidence of this in parallel passages would probably foil the most accomplished hounds of
research. Whatever aid he had from other authors, Law was
not any man's disciple. He was saved from that by the
breadth of his reading and by his urgent sense of obligation
to relieve the religious destitution of his own time. He always felt strongly one conviction which he states succinctly
in his tract, *The Spirit of Prayer* (1749): "Hold this therefore as a certain truth, that the heresy of heresies is a worldly
spirit." "Herein," he says, "consists the apostasy and degen-

[5] *Selected Mystical Writings of William Law* (London: Daniel,
1938). Konrad Minkner in *Die Stufenfolge des mystischen Erlebnisses
bei William Law* (Munich: 1939) offers a wide range of similar background information. Minkner, while stressing the contribution of
Böhme, finds a mystical element in the earlier writings and indicates
a mystical significance in the "great change" of 1720.

eracy of the church." It is the attack upon this heresy that
gives continuity to the whole of his work. The extreme expression of it is seen in an early treatise entitled *The Absolute Unlawfulness of Stage Entertainments* (1726). Here he
asserts unconditionally that "the playhouse is the porch of
hell . . .: a play is the devil's triumph, a sacrifice performed
to his glory." Gibbon refers to this, along with his later
mysticism, as among those "sallies of religious frenzy" which
injure Law's record as "a wit and a scholar."

Law delights in enforcing his arguments by fictitious examples, and his books abound in character sketches drawn,
not without exaggeration, from a fund of knowledge of the
people of his time, but intended to present types rather than
individuals. "Many of his portraits," says Gibbon, "are not
unworthy of the pen of a La Bruyère." The reference is to
the French master of the character sketch (d. 1696). As in
the case of Bunyan, the characters are either good or bad.
There are some incomplete saints with grave but curable
faults, but there are no neutrals. Those whom common opinion would regard as neutral are in Law's austere judgment
condemned. Theirs is the fate of the Laodiceans. Law shares
Bunyan's attitude to people of the Pliable and By-ends sort,
who would serve God and mammon. But Law is not indebted to Bunyan, and his characters are not, like Bunyan's,
revealed in invented conversation. As with the typical character sketch of La Bruyère or John Earle or Samuel Butler,
they are described directly. Law gives classical names to
these creations. We may question whether this is done in
order to divert his readers from attempting to identify them
with individuals in the author's circle of acquaintances. His
use of this method of illustration is masterly. But he is almost
never content to let the character sketch make its own impression. The moral is earnestly and often argumentatively
enforced.

III

The *Serious Call* may be regarded as a continuation and application of the theme of the *Christian Perfection;* but it has found, and deserved, more readers than the earlier treatise. It is important to note that Law uses terms like "perfection" and "devotion" to characterize not the life of a limited class of saints but that to which all Christians are obligated to commit themselves. "As there is but one faith and one baptism, so there is but one piety, and one perfection, that is common to all orders of Christians." This perfection is not presented negatively as the exclusion of sin, but positively as the performance of necessary duties and the exercise of "holy tempers" in all states of life. Men in cloisters cannot attain to more than this; Christians in general dare not strive for less. God may be merciful to an inferior piety, but if this is our choice and aim it becomes impiety. Christianity is not a school of mundane virtue but a new life, a dedication of soul and body, under the impulse of the divine grace revealed in Scripture. It involves renunciation of the ways of the world, a constant prayerfulness, and imitation of the example of Christ in preparation for union with Him hereafter. We have no time for worldly frivolity: in this life we are as a man crossing a river upon a rope, who dares not look around to enjoy the scenery. It would be small perfection to pursue this piety if all others about us were pursuing it, but to be "heavenly-minded among the worldly" is the test of true devotion. Such is Law's prescription for the Christian life as it is set forth in the *Practical Treatise Upon Christian Perfection.*

The *Serious Call* begins with a fresh definition of devotion. This consists in neither public nor private prayer, though it includes both. It is simply a life devoted to God. The manner and objects of the Christian's prayer must conform to God's glory, and this rule applies to all our actions no less than to our prayers. Those who are devout in church and undevout in their ordinary actions justly invite the scorn of the worldly. Here we meet the character of Julius, who if he should be absent from church would be assumed to be sick, but on other occasions is the companion of the silliest worldlings in their frivolous pleasures. Law even asserts that frequent churchgoing is not so much as mentioned in Scripture, a statement to which Charles Wesley later with reason objected. Better justified is the positive statement of the matter: "That religion or devotion that is to govern the ordinary actions of our life, is to be found in almost every verse of Scripture." Eusebius, who buys books of devotion, and discourses about church festivals and saintly men, can hardly be said to be better than Leo, who hardly knows the difference between a Jew and a Christian, if he lives as Leo does, equally prizing the riches, pleasures and honors of the world.

Why is it, Law asks, that most Christians fall so far short of the devout life? It is because they have no sincere intention to please God in all their actions. The prevalence of the vice of swearing among men and the addiction of women to vanity and idleness exhibit this lack of devout intention. The clergyman who is resolved to please God in all his actions will show a burning zeal to save souls; the tradesman with such intention will be a saint in his shop; the gentleman of birth and fortune will abandon wasteful folly and spend all he can in charitable relief.

Law is saying that we are not, only because we do not want to be, good Christians. Undoubtedly he lays the emphasis upon the will. He will have something to say later of regeneration. But here his exhortation assumes the ability of sinners to reclaim themselves by decision and resolution. This is what John Wesley came to regard as a fatal defect in Law's conception of religion. In those days of anguish before his conversion, when Peter Böhler had taught him a doctrine of justification by faith, Wesley turned reproachfully upon Law. On May 14, 1738, ten days before his Aldersgate experience, he wrote to his former adviser an accusing letter.[6] Law had failed to point out to his distressed inquirer the way of faith and salvation. He questions whether Law has truly experienced the faith that saves.

In passages such as this we miss the evangel of Paul, Luther and Wesley. Law does not guard his argument by any reference to grace. "We have the power," he says; we simply lack the intention. He goes on to stress the point that we must "strive," not merely halfheartedly "seek," to enter in at the strait gate. God's mercy is offered only to our best endeavors. He recites the last despairful thoughts of a worldly man summoned by death who too late realizes that his plight is due to the fact that he has never embraced a devout intention and now, on the brink of torment, longs in vain for one year more in which to reverse his course. This character is named Penitens. The implication is that a deathbed repentance is vain.

Law does not pamper us with a comfortable piety. There are no excuses and no exceptions. Just as to the Christian every place is holy because God is there, so every part of his life is to be offered unto God. Not only is the clerical profession a holy calling, but also what is called worldly business is to be made holy unto the Lord. Like Luther, but with

[6] *Letters of the Reverend John Wesley,* edited by J. Telford (London: Methuen, 1931), I, 238 ff. Wesley elsewhere has both gratitude and criticism for Law. He states that on reading the *Serious Call* (for which he paid-five shillings in May, 1732) he had objections on almost every page, but also that it had given him a fuller realization of the love of God. When he read Law on the *New Birth* (1739) he was moved to quote Shakespeare (with a slight variation): "O what a fall is there." (*Journal of John Wesley,* edited by N. Curnock [London: 1910], II, 207). Wesley republished most of the *Serious Call* in the Christian Library.

more austerity, he preaches the sacredness of lay vocations. Holiness should pervade all callings, and we should engage in them only as those who are in preparation for the life to come. Human activities, apart from this high end, if we are to believe the Scriptures, are to be reckoned as "bubbles, vapors, dreams and shadows."

The pitiable case of the man devoted to business for its own sake, and caught in its treadmill, is illustrated in the character of Calidus. He has been engaged for thirty years in building up his trade and his fortune. He drinks in a tavern at night to drive thoughts of business out of his head and enable him to sleep. He works mentally at his business when rising and going to his office. "His prayers are a short ejaculation or two, which he never misses in stormy and tempestuous weather, because he has always something or other at sea." Always in a hurry, he says he would have been dead long ago had he not spent his week ends in the country. He is rich enough to retire, but fears that if he should quit his business he would grow melancholy. As for religion, he can claim to have been no friend of heretics, courteous to the minister and an occasional contributor to the charity schools. Most of the trading class, Law supposes, are too much like Calidus. They fail to observe the apostolic rule: "With good will doing service as unto the Lord and not to men."

In Law's teaching, the most lawful employment becomes sinful unless men engage in it to the glory of God. The glory of God as the norm of conduct is one of his favorite themes. This fact has been especially stressed in another connection by Andrew Murray. In an introduction to Law's *Address to the Clergy*[1] he has likened our author in his emphasis on the glory of God and our dependence upon Him

---

[1] *The Power of the Spirit and Other Extracts from the Writings of William Law* (New York: 1895), p. xiii.

to John Calvin, whose teaching at other points Law sharply rejects. This concept of the divine glory rebukes all the perverse pretensions that vitiate the life of action. Vanity, pride, covetousness and ambition are sins that beset men of business and pollute even their prayers and alms. Law warns us against supposing that a man may be proud in some things and humble in others. A man vain of his estate or his learning, or ambitious in his views, may disregard his dress, but this is not from humility. "We must eat and drink, and dress and discourse, according to the sobriety of the Christian spirit." All should be governed by the spirit of devotion. Though eating is "one of the lowest actions of our lives," common to us with all animals, yet it should be related to piety and accompanied by sincere and not merely perfunctory prayer.

IV

A considerable section of the book (chapters v–ix) is especially designed to guide in the paths of devotion those who are "free from the necessity of labor or employments." Law is much at home with the well-to-do leisured class, and it is noteworthy that he regards it as numerous—a "great part of the world." They are those to whom much is given and of whom much will be required. Law is their monitor, not their flatterer. Since they have been given full opportunity to seek perfection, the honor of God and the good of their neighbors, they must devote themselves to study the arts and methods of devotion, to make their souls the object of their daily care and to be wise and holy in the use of all their money. Here, as frequently elsewhere, Law argues for the all-comprehending character of devotion from considerations of reason and nature. The Gospel "only requires a life of the highest reason." We are enjoined "to use this world as in reason it ought to be used, to live in such tempers as are the glory of intelligent beings, to walk in such wisdom as exalts our nature. "This applies not to some occasions only, but to all. Those who argue for the admission of indulgences and vanities and for the misuse of time and money plead for rebellion against our nature and against God who has given us reason to be the rule and measure of all our life.

In this appeal to reason we seem to hear an echo of the voice of Hooker. But in the century between Hooker and Law reason had come to be the keynote of many a religious treatise. The Cambridge Platonists, Jeremy Taylor and John Locke, had come and gone, and, with variations in detail, many were convinced of what Locke called "the reasonableness of Christianity."[8] In Law's case there is no thought of reason excluding revelation. At the opening of *Christian Perfection* he wrote eloquently of the light of revelation shed upon human darkness and perplexity. And in the present passage he appeals to Scripture with its "exhortations to be wise and reasonable." But there was a practical point in his emphasis here upon the reasonableness of the devout life. He is especially addressing a privileged class of people who have read the books then in vogue and in whose talk "reason" is a kind of social password. Like St. Paul (as reported) on Mars Hill, Law places himself on common ground with his audience in order to move them to his own chosen position. We are agreed, he argues in substance, that we ought to be reasonable; it is reasonable to commit to God the whole of life and not only shreds and fragments of it; hence you must adopt a course of complete dedication.

By carefully marshaled arguments, the possessors of "es-

---

[8] "His [Locke's] work, *The Reasonableness of Christianity* typifies the tone of the writers on Christian evidences for the next half century" (A. S. Farrar, *A Critical History of Free Thought* [New York: 1882], p. 125).

tates and fortunes" are urged to make a religious use of
them. It is life itself that we are to devote to God, and for
those who have wealth the manner of using it is a large part
of life. Moreover, property may become a great means of
doing good. To waste it is not only to lose the opportunity
of ministering to the distressed but also "that which might
purchase for ourselves everlasting treasures in heaven." This
is one of the most explicit statements of a doctrine of merit
and reward for good works that crops out frequently in
Law's writings; but the language is partly that of the Sermon on the Mount. In support of the same view he quotes at
length from the judgment scene of Matthew 25 and comments: "There is therefore no salvation but in the performance of these good works." This end is not to be achieved by
occasional spurts of help to the poor or sick but only by
habitual and lifelong exercise of such charities. As there is no
middle way between pride and humility, so there is no justifiable middle ground between a limited and a complete devotion of worldly goods.

In this connection one must beware of "the indiscreet and
dangerous use of innocent and lawful things." Law here introduces the two sisters, Flavia and Miranda, probably the
best remembered of his characters. "Under the names of
Flavia and Miranda," says Gibbon, "he admirably described
my two aunts, the heathen and the Christian sister."[9] Hester
Gibbon, the Christian sister, chose, as her learned nephew
puts the matter, "a life of devotion and celibacy." As we
have already noted, she was later to be a member of Law's
household; she survived him and lived to a great age. When
Gibbon wrote his autobiography (1789) his good aunt was
eighty-five years old. Perhaps he forgot that when Law
wrote (1728) she was only twenty-four and could hardly
have achieved the prodigious works ascribed to Miranda.

[9] Gibbon, *op. cit.*, p. 17.

Gibbon also tells us that his heathen aunt, Catherine, became Mrs. Edward Elliston and had four children. But Law makes the pair "two maiden sisters." The father of the Gibbon sisters died in 1737, eight years after the *Serious Call* appeared, but in the book the two ladies had "buried their parents twenty years ago." Noting some of this evidence, J. H. Overton has observed:

> If Gibbon means by this that the two ladies in question unconsciously sat for their portraits, the presumption is very strong against it. . . . It was singularly unlike Law to hold up as a model of perfection one who would of course read what he wrote. . . . On the other hand, Law had far too much Christian feeling to gibbet the daughter of his friend and benefactor under the character of Flavia. . . . It was Miranda who was to be the model for Miss Gibbon . . . not Miss Gibbon who was to be the model for Miranda.[10]

Gibbon may have meant merely that his aunts answered to the description of these characters; whatever he meant we must discard the notion that Law was drawing their portraits.

Flavia on her modest fortune manages to be fashionable and constant in attendance at places of amusement. She talks against heretics and generally goes to church. She likes a sermon against vanity which she can apply to another lady. She occasionally tosses half a crown to charity, complaining that the length of her milliner's bill forbids a larger gift. When three months later there is a new appeal for charity she applauds it but, remembering her former generosity, refrains from giving anything. She is very apprehensive of giving amiss and is convinced that the poor are dishonest. She buys books of humor and once in a while *borrows* a book of piety, but it must be a short one. On Sundays she entertains her guests with talk of the current lampoons, plays and card games, and with malicious gossip. She is,

[10] *Life of William Law* (London: 1881), pp. 104 f.

however, so virtuously anxious for the sanctity of Sunday that "she has turned a poor old widow out of her house as a profane wretch for mending her clothes on the Sunday night." Becoming statistically sarcastic, Law tells us how many suits of clothes she will have worn if she lives ten years more; how many years in bed, how many in vain pursuits, make up her span of life; and estimates that she will spend on herself six thousand pounds, less a few shillings, crowns and half crowns that have gone in "accidental charities." To be sure, Law seems to feel that she is a little unusual:

Now though the irregular trifling spirit of this character belongs, I hope, to but a few people, yet many may learn some instruction from it, and perhaps see something of their own spirit in it.

But how different is that "sober and reasonable Christian," her sister Miranda! With no pretensions to the role of a fine lady, she follows Christ "in humility, charity, devotion, piety and heavenly affections." She divides her fortune with "several other poor people," making herself but one of those whose poverty is relieved by it. She is early at prayer and never has a dull half day. She labors with her hands to clothe the needy. She is abstinent and devout at meals and does not suffer from "a load of flesh." The Scriptures are her daily study; in them she learns the laws of her life. The only books she buys are guides to devotion, and the religious life is the subject of her conversation. Her numerous charities include the education of poor children; doubling the wages of sick laborers; and a special care for the families of wasteful reprobates, by which means she has brought one profligate to repentance. Law calls this tenderness of affection for abandoned sinners the highest evidence of a Godlike soul. She has actually bought three children from their unfit parents and raised them in her house with the result that the parents are converted by one of them, who is to enter holy orders. She relieves those who suffer crippling losses, the aged, the sick and the wandering beggars, never treating them with disregard or aversion. Since she prays for grace beyond her own deserving, she does kindness to those who least deserve it.

Law represents this life of unreserved and industrious benevolence as the pattern for Christians of the privileged class. But as he proceeds to apply its lessons he takes into consideration the need of adjusting conduct to variant circumstances. Particularly is this necessary in the case of a woman who is married and may not offend her husband. If the husband disapproves of plain apparel she is at least to adopt it as soon as he can be so reformed as to be persuaded to permit it. With respect to dress, food and drink, no rules can be made that are equally applicable to all. But we must let religion teach us to drink only for refreshment and health and to clothe ourselves with the object of hiding our nakedness and protecting our bodies from the weather. Children, like married women in being under restraint, may be unable to avoid concessions to the vanity of their parents. They must bear this as a cross until they are at liberty to follow the higher counsels of Christ. There is no compromise here in principle: all are to live in the spirit of Miranda if they cannot imitate all her acts.

Law advocated clerical celibacy, and he here introduces a plea for celibate religious communities. A selection from a tract of Eusebius of Caesarea is quoted, in which that ecclesiastical historian refers to the two ways of Christian living, one the perfect way of ascetic devotion, the other the secondary piety of ordinary family life. A notable suggestion follows in which Law anticipates Pusey's revival of ascetic orders in the Church of England:

If therefore persons of either sex, moved with the life of Miranda and desirous of perfection, should unite themselves into little societies, professing voluntary poverty, virginity, retirement and devotion, living upon bare necessaries, that some might be relieved by their charities and be blessed by their prayers, such persons would be so far from being chargeable with any superstition, or blind devotion, that they might be justly said to restore that piety which was the boast and glory of the church when its greatest saints were alive.

This seems inconsistent with his earlier statement that Christian perfection calls no one to a cloister; and he here makes no explanation of the seeming reversal of judgment. Later (chapter xxiv) he represents the life of virginity and voluntary poverty as not indeed necessary but distinctly advantageous to true devotion. Obviously his own practice approached what he here proposes for others. The household established at King's Cliffe may be considered, in terms of early monasticism, a kind of miniature "double monastery."

The treatise now proceeds to give guidance for devotion to "all orders and ranks of men and women." The range of employment with which he shows acquaintance is, however, limited. The irreligion and indolence of the educated is stigmatized in Fulvius, who has taken degrees in the university and thereafter refuses all responsibilities, including that of marriage. Reproof of this "unreasonable" conduct is mingled with suitable exhortation. The soldier or tradesman is no less obligated to be devout than the priest. Young women must either be saintly virgins or wives and mothers, holy and sober in family duties. Young gentlemen must acknowledge that their only business is to distinguish themselves by good works. Two chapters (xi and xii) are filled with proofs that devotion is the sole basis of true happiness, and characters are introduced to indicate the misery of the worldly. Flatus (who has been unjustifiably identified with Edward Gibbon, the historian's father) is a type of restless pursuer of happiness. He passes rapidly through stages of fine dress, dueling, town entertainments, hunting ("he leaped more hedges and ditches than had ever been known in so short a time"), experiments in architecture, the study of Italian grammar and (too late, one would suppose) dieting and training himself to run. He experiences only anxieties and delusions. Yet many people, honestly reviewing their lives in maturity, would find that they have followed as many forms of unrewarding folly. The female counterpart of Flatus is Feliciana, whose series of fashions and vanities have never given her a pleasant day. We are told of the gluttony and intemperance of Succus, who in his cups "talks of the excellency of the English constitution" and on occasion condemns the town rakes only because they never have a regular meal. These are but illustrations of "the emptiness and error of all worldly happiness"; it is contrasted with that happiness which is found in "the hopes and expectations of religion."

V

We must consider briefly Law's extended directions for the conduct of the devotional life. He sets down a detailed program of daily prayer. Early rising for prayer is enjoined: morning slothfulness is "odious in the sight of heaven." Every new day should be received as a resurrection from death. Some form of prayer is to be used, but rigorous inflexibility is to be avoided. Prayer should be practiced kneeling, with the eyes closed, and in a place set apart for that purpose. It should begin with expressions of the attributes of God, to make us sensible of his greatness and power. Law gives large importance to the chanting or singing of the Psalms. In the words of Overton, "Law was himself passionately fond of music, and he held the somewhat untenable position that every one can sing." He added a music room to the Hall

Yard House, with an organ, on which Miss Gibbon played.[11] He regards psalm singing as the natural expression of thanksgiving. In this connection he is led to reflect on the union of soul and body by which the bodily action of singing affects the soul, and to condemn both the quietism that would reject such aids and the superstition that would make religion consist in bodily actions alone. He would select psalms that "wonderfully set forth the glory of God," and employ the imagination to visualize the heavenly chorus.

Having begun the day with these exercises, the devout Christian is to observe a second season of prayer at nine o'clock—the "third hour," in Scripture language. The theme proposed is humility, "a true and just sense of our weakness, misery and sin." Law's treatment of these topics serves as a corrective of the former assertion that "we have the power" to be good. He now states: "In our natural state we are entirely without any power." We "can only act by a power that is every moment lent us by God."[12] Some paragraphs here approach Reformation conceptions of sin. He holds that, abusing the gift of reason, "we reason ourselves into all kinds of miseries." And when he goes on to stress the shame and guilt of sin his language is close to that of Luther and Wesley: "Nothing less has been required to take away the guilt of our sins, than the sufferings and death of the Son of God." Yet it is hardly surprising that these evangelical passages made no clear impression at the time upon the anxious young leader of the Holy Club. They are quite subordinated to an instruction in humility. "Let a man," Law presently adds, "when he is most delighted with his own figure, look upon a crucifix. . . ." Humility may escape us,

[11] Overton, *op. cit.*, pp. 106, 235.

[12] This language may reflect the influence of Malebranche, whom Law had begun to read with admiration; but we have quoted above a similar passage from Hooker: "perpetual aid and concurrence of that Supreme Cause" (p. 74).

as it escapes Caecus, who admires humble people and is blind to his own vanity.

The cultivation of humility requires a course of training. That education which enforces the principles of Socrates and Pythagoras falls short of Christian instruction. Emulation between pupils is "nothing else than a refinement upon envy," that black and venomous passion. In Paternus, the wise father here introduced, who "lived 200 years ago," some have thought they discerned the father of Law himself. He is represented as discoursing to his ten-year-old son in a garden concerning God, who is Creator of the universe and Father of all nations, and at once judge and guide of the soul. These religious concepts should control the child's mind. Paternus explains why Latin and Greek are needed as keys to ancient wisdom, and enjoins truth and plainness of speech, a sober garb, temperance, the despising of human glory and the cultivation of unfeigned love.

Our author next turns his sarcasm against the fashionable education of girls, which is directly opposed to humility. He employs the character of Matilda, the vain mother, and balances with her the saintly Eusebia. Matilda's' eldest daughter has died at twenty from tight lacing of her corset at the command of her mother. Eusebia has her five daughters and her maids daily observe appointed hours of prayer and spend the rest of their time in good works and innocent diversions. She especially inculcates humility and warns her offspring against fashionable vanities and every form of pride, including pride in their own virtues. Law's mother, Margaret Farmery, was doubtless an exemplary Christian, but those who would identify her with Eusebia have to reckon with the widely different life situations of the two. (For one thing, there were eight boys and three girls in the Law family.)

For the noon, or sixth, hour, the theme of devotion recommended is universal love. Though the Golden Rule is a rule of justice, only universal love can comply with it. All human beings must be embraced within our circle of love: "It is not Christian love till it is the love of all." Law makes an eloquent and logical plea for a love not bounded or conditioned by the worthiness of its human objects. God loves us not because we are good but in order to make us so. Hence our love of virtue should imply not abhorrence but compassion toward those who lack it—"as when we see the miseries of a hospital." Intercessory prayer gives devout expression to this universal love; and this is an intercession not only mutual among Christians but for all mankind. In turn, the act of intercession arouses love in us: "Nothing makes us love a man like praying for him."

Ouranius, "a holy priest" in a poor village, is portrayed as the exemplary intercessor. He takes his place with the great pastors who stand out in English literature, from Bede's description of St. Aidan through Chaucer's "poor parson of a town," Fuller's "good preacher" (a portrait of the Puritan, William Perkins) and Goldsmith's village parson, who "lured to brighter worlds and led the way." Ouranius is very different from any of these. Overton is justified in suggesting points at which he resembles Law himself,[13] including an early natural haughtiness and contempt for foolish people, which had been overcome by the practice of the devout life. From regarding his little parish as a prison from which he could mentally escape by sitting in his study and reading Homer, Ouranius has come to be the eager and happy servant of all. It is not clear what has led him to be a great intercessor. What Law is interested in stressing is that his prayers have inspired his works.

It would strangely delight you to see with what spirit he converses, with what tenderness he reproves, with what affection

13 Overton, *op. cit.*, p. 258.

he exhorts, and with what vigor he preaches; and it is all owing to this because he reproves, exhorts and preaches to those for whom he first prays to God.

"Resignation to the divine pleasure" is the topic for the ninth hour, or three o'clock. We are not only to submit to God's providence but to accept it cheerfully and thankfully. We contemplate, first, God's general providence; and devotion requires uncomplaining acceptance of political changes, of the seasons and weather, even of the calamities and persecutions that God permits for his own ends. We are not herein to call evil good and good evil. But in devout resignation there lies "a truly religious greatness of mind." Resignation involves, secondly, a thankful acceptance of our own lot, which would seem fitting to us if we could see all that God sees. As a sick man would be unreasonable to demand the treatment proper for another's different disease, so we are foolish to envy another his circumstances. Modern psychology explores different approaches to this problem of the acceptance of the world and of our own limitations. Law's approach is that of happy resignation, in assured reliance upon God's good intent.

Six o'clock, the twelfth hour of the day, is to be observed with self-examination and confession of the day's sins. There is nothing original in this bringing oneself to account at nightfall: it had been advocated by the Stoics, and in Puritan diaries it is a commonplace. Wesley caught the idea not from Law but from Jeremy Taylor. With earlier Christian writers, Law stresses the element of repentance; but we must review in detail that whereof we ought to repent. It is noteworthy, and surprising, that Law has nothing to say of confession to a spiritual adviser; the rehearsal of offenses is a purely private matter. The stains upon the soul are laid bare before God, to whom all sin is odious, and there is to be no self-righteous comparison of ourselves with other sinners. Finally (and this too is old advice), we are to commit ourselves to sleep with a prayer on the subject of death. "Represent to your imagination that your bed is your grave," allowing no further opportunity of doing good.

Such, according to William Law, is the devout life; he reiterates in his concluding chapter that it is also the life of reason. It is not, he argues, a course of cowardice or bigotry, but

there is nothing wise or great or noble in an human spirit, but rightly to know and heartily worship and adore the great God that is the support and life of all spirits, whether in heaven or on earth.

VI

How shall we evaluate this earnest and impressive book? It has often been criticized, both for some things that it contains and for some that it omits. Perhaps we have a right to say that Law relies too much on a round of religious acts. His routine of devotion appears a little crowded, and might tend to become mechanical and oppressive. We have known people whose dedication is unreserved who manage with a great deal less of timed and regulated piety. Their devotion finds play in all their work and thought. That religion should find such expression is indeed a principle dear to Law; but he so points up the occasions of private devotion as in some degree to lose contact with workaday Christian living. In the perfections of Miranda and Ouranius there seems to lurk the danger of being righteous overmuch, the danger of religious artificiality. Yet a patient reading of the book will show that he tried to guard against this and all other sorts of insincerity.

The limitations of the *Serious Call* were partly imposed by the author's circumstances. Dr. R. Newton Flew has referred to his "remoteness from ordinary life." He further, perhaps not quite justifiably, holds that Law has not grasped Luther's conception of vocation.[14] The relative neglect of the church as the inspiration and the theater of action of the devout life may have been the result of his detachment from the established Church of England. Again, the book is designed to redirect those especially exposed to the perils of wealth and leisure. We ought not to blame Law for assuming the role of mentor to the rich: somebody ought to minister to them. But in such a ministry there should be an attempt to introduce the rich to the poor, and with the latter Law had only a distant, if sympathetic, acquaintance. From modern standpoints, the book is weak on the social side of Christianity. It offers no guidance to political ethics and, with all its emphasis upon charity, has no concern for the reform of public life and economic abuses. Religion for Law thus appears as almost purely an individual matter, with no outlet in social experience and public causes such as made the Evangelical movement a power in the earth.

Law has been criticized, too, for his theological presuppositions, his one-sided emphasis on good works, his lack of stress on Scripture as the resource of the devout, his failure to assert the transforming and enabling power of grace appropriated by faith. These criticisms naturally occur to those of evangelical heritage, as well as to those under the influence of Pascal or Kierkegaard or of leading contemporary theologians. If we look closely enough, however, we shall see that some of the allegedly missing elements are present, and merely obscured by matters more congenial to Law's mind. It is fair to say that he lacks theological profundity;

[14] *The Idea of Perfection in Christian Theology* (London: Oxford University Press, 1934), pp. 300 f.

he fails in this book to plumb the depths of man's plight and moral agony.

That the book has had a wide and sustained appeal to earnest people is, however, a fact which these criticisms do not explain. George Whitefield testified that when at last he found an edition cheap enough for his purse, it worked mightily upon his soul. Dr. Samuel Johnson, certainly an intellectually respectable witness, called it "the finest piece of hortatory theology in any language." Johnson had been, he confesses, "a sort of lax talker against religion" and he opened the book expecting it to prove a dull one. "But," he adds, "I found Law quite an over-match for me; and this was the first occasion of my thinking in earnest." Gibbon notes that its precepts are rigid but founded upon the Gospel, and that it will kindle to a flame any spark of piety in the reader's mind. An unnamed eighteenth-century clergyman, half-discouraged by the hardy vices of his parishioners, presented copies of the *Serious Call* to each of them, and thereafter declared (1771) that they had transformed the parish.[15]

The influence of the *Serious Call* has been acknowledged by many who have criticized it in detail. That it did exert a marked influence alike upon Wesley and Methodism, upon Henry Venn, Thomas Scott and their Claphamite and Evangelical associates, and upon Newman and the Oxford movement[16] is not open to doubt. Late in the nineteenth century it was discriminatingly praised by Sir Leslie Stephen,[17] and its characters were brought to fresh notice by the Scottish

[15] Other similar testimonies are reported by J. N. Overton, *op. cit.*, pp. 109 ff.

[16] Y. Brilioth, *The Anglican Revival* (London: Longmans, 1925), pp. 18 f.; C. F. Harrold, *John Henry Newman* (London: Longmans, 1945), p. 4.

[17] *English Thought in the Eighteenth Century* (1876; 3rd edition, London, 1902), II, 394 ff.

Evangelical, Alexander Whyte,[18] who afterwards paid a pious visit to Law's home at King's Cliffe.[19] G. B. Morgan, the modern editor (as "G. Moreton") of Law's *Works* (1892–93), calls the *Serious Call* Law's "fame-piece, if not . . . his masterpiece." Its appearance in the Everyman series (1906), and in later editions, is evidence of a continued demand for it in our century. As this is written, a new American edition is in prospect.

From Wesley down, many readers have expressed delight over the style of the book. In a late sermon Wesley commends it as "hardly excelled in the English tongue for beauty of expression. . . ." It must, I think, be admitted that Law's desire to enforce a lesson leads to a certain amount of repetition, which becomes at times a little wearisome. In general, however, the style is marked by spiritual elevation, natural dignity and simple directness; it is quite free from meretricious ornament and dated literary fashion. Yet it would be a mistake to suppose that the secret of the book's appeal lies in its stylistic excellence. Doubtless its satirical passages have added to its popularity, but it is not primarily a satirical work. Its very title is forbidding to the secular mind. We may attribute its sustained attraction for readers mainly to the tremendous earnestness of its affirmation of religion and morality. This quality in it made Keble resent Froude's remark that it is "a clever book"; as well might one say, he replied, that the Judgment Day would be a pretty sight. Sir Leslie Stephen finds its greatness in the fact that the author "believes what he professes, and believes it in a downright sense."[20]

Dr. Overton is a little misleading when he argues that it

[18] *Characters and Characteristics of William Law* (London: 1892).

[19] G. F. Barbour, *Life of Alexander Whyte* (London: 1924), pp. 380 ff.

[20] Sir Leslie Stephen, *op. cit.*, p. 398.

is not, properly speaking, a devotional book but simply a "call" to devotion.[21] It not only exhorts, but presents a plan of devotional exercises. Most readers, however, have not followed the plan. Perhaps no one has ever closely followed it. But many, it cannot be doubted, even of those who have dissented from Law's theology, have responded to the call. In our own day, when secularity and spirituality are in mortal combat in the world, the *Serious Call*, with its summons to an uncompromising dedication of life, may again reinforce the agencies of the Spirit.

[21] Overton, *op. cit.*, p. 117.

JOHN WESLEY'S JOURNAL

JOHN WESLEY'S JOURNAL

Few men have been more industrious than Wesley in keeping records of their own experiences and doings. Nehemiah Curnock, editor of the standard edition of the *Journal*,[1] lists eighteen fragments of private diaries which he wrote in abbreviated script or cipher between 1725 and 1791. A number of these, embracing diary material of nearly fifty years, are lost. Curnock has made extensive use of five of them as material for the expansion of the *Journal* itself. The careful editor has been partially frustrated, however, by patches of a shorthand not now understood, as well as by a variety of abbreviations and cipher symbols not yet fully interpreted. Wesley kept the diaries as a private record, but utilized them in the *Journal*, of which he published the first portion in 1739. "It was," he writes in the preface of this publication,

in pursuance of an advice given by Bp. Taylor in his *Rules for Holy Living and Holy Dying*, that about fifteen years ago I began to take a more exact Account than I had done before, of the manner wherein I spent my Time, writing down how I had employed every Hour.

Jeremy Taylor had advised (as had Stoic philosophers of old) a scrutiny of the day's actions before sleep. This was, in fact, the practice of many a Puritan diarist. "The diary," says William Haller, "was the Puritan's confessional."[2] John Wesley's *Journal* is in part a record of this kind. In its earlier

[1] *Journal of John Wesley*, edited by N. Curnock (London: 1909–16), 8 vols.
[2] *The Rise of Puritanism* (New York: Columbia University Press, 1938), p. 38.

sections we see little else than an anxious and intense young man taking stock of his own soul. Later, when the inner problem is essentially solved and Wesley is at full career in his program of activity, the area of interest moves outward to incidents of the rising movement. In the later years the "confessional" element is rarely discoverable. If he then talks about himself it is apt to be in such a remark as: "In seventy years I have not lost one night's sleep," or "I walk slower, particularly uphill." When, at eighty-six, this slowing of his uphill pace comes to his attention, he is probably less perturbed by it than at twenty-three he had been when he inquired of himself one Saturday night: "Have I loved women or company more than God?" The laborious introvert gradually gives place to the energetic and masterful leader of an expanding movement. In both stages the record is faithful and illuminating. Whether Wesley tells us about himself or about his work, travels and contemporaries, he is writing one of the most animated and important records we have of eighteenth-century life.

It was in defense of his reputation that Wesley was first led to publish a selection of his private records. After his return from Georgia, and after his conversion experience in 1738, he had been attacked in a sworn statement by Captain Robert Williams, a Georgia planter, who, it is believed, disliked Wesley because of the latter's opposition to the slave trade. Williams had alleged that Wesley had been culpably imprudent in his relations with parishioners in Georgia, and that he had slipped bail in a Georgia court. Years later, in a personal letter to Williams of August 3, 1742, Wesley accuses him of "gross, wilful, palpable untruth."[3] To this attack we owe the appearance of the first of the twenty sections in which, at intervals of Wesley's life, the *Journal* was

[3] *The Letters of the Reverend John Wesley*, edited by J. Telford, II, 6–7.

to appear in print. It is of some interest that Wesley after his conversion was to this extent concerned to defend his conduct before his conversion.

II

The *Journal* opens with an account of the author's voyage to America. With his brother Charles and two other religious young men he boarded a ship at Gravesend October 14, 1735. It is an hour of destiny when the thirty-two-year-old Oxford scholar and fellow of Lincoln College, formerly a close student and lover of Horace, Homer and Shakespeare, more recently a prominent member of the group called by him "Our Company" and by scoffers "the Holy Club," undertakes the perilous and distressful winter passage to the New World. Why did he go? He gives two motives, and sufficiently indicates which was dominant. Just before leaving (October 10) he writes:

My chief motive is the hope of saving my own soul. I hope to learn the sense of the Gospel by preaching it to the heathen.

He went to preach to Indians, but to do this in order that his own salvation would be secure. The same primary anxiety about his own status is seen when after his return he reflects on the American experience in these words: "I went to America to convert Indians; but O! who shall convert me?" It is noteworthy also that the conversion or salvation he craves involved "learning the sense of the Gospel"; he was to find his way to this, but not yet.

The voyage to America, then, was a part of the pilgrimage of Wesley's soul. Turned back after starting by bad weather, the ship finally left Cowes, December 10, and was soon on stormy seas. It was eight weeks later, on February 6, 1736, about eight in the morning, that Wesley first set foot on American ground, but on a little island off Savannah. We see him on shipboard strangely immune from the prevailing seasickness, making gruel and bringing it to the sick. This part of the record is from the portion of the diary unpublished by Wesley. He also engaged the passengers personally in religious conversation, and conducted Holy Communion. The names of those to whose souls he privately ministered are given: most of them were women. He received generally a favorable response. There was much discussion with Charles Wesley and their companions, Delamotte and Ingham. They were not always in agreement. On January 26 he wrote in his diary: "8. Sat with Charles and Ingham. Charles perverse."

Throughout the long passage, storm succeeded storm. The tempest disturbed, not his digestion, but his soul:

> About nine the sea broke over us from stem to stern. . . . About eleven I lay down in the great cabin and in a short time fell asleep, though very uncertain that I should awake alive, and much ashamed of my unwillingness to die (January 17, 1736).

Another day a wave struck him on the deck and knocked him down. A still more violent gale followed; the winds roared and whistled, the ship rocked and trembled. Wesley was afraid.

There was a group of devout Christians on board who through all this showed no sign of fear. They were German-speaking Moravians, who after a stay in England were on their way to Georgia. Almost as soon as Wesley saw that they were aboard, at Gravesend, he had begun to give three hours a day to the German language. He was later to study Spanish and French, less for scholarly than for missionary purposes. With characteristic thoroughness he made grammars of all these languages to aid his studies (November 26, 1736). During the heavy weather he went to a Moravian service to find out their secret. At that moment a wave "split

the mainsail in pieces." The English-speaking passengers
screamed; the Moravians continued to sing. In answer to
Wesley's questions they said simply that they were not
afraid to die. Wesley at once made an example of them to
the others. In Georgia he was to enjoy association with
August Gottlieb Spangenberg, leader of the Moravians.
Wesley consulted him regarding his own conduct. He star-
tled Wesley by asking: "Do you know Christ has saved
you?" Wesley would be further stimulated by the Moravians on the way to his conversion. On the voyage he had
been much perplexed by the religious state of a certain Mrs.
Hawkins. He now asked Spangenberg about this case. The
Moravian quoted in Latin from the *Imitation of Christ:*
"Avoid all good women and commend them to God." Wesley realized that the advice was applicable, at least in a
measure, to the situation. He would have been happier in
Georgia if he had heeded the words more constantly:
"*Omnes bonas mulieres devita.*"

Dr. Curnock remarks in this connection that all Wesley's
friends were treated as pupils (Vol. I, p. 182). What is
more, we may say that he sought friends only in an at-
mosphere of religion. When someone tries to engage him in
secular conversation, he responds (in substance) with this
illustration: Suppose you were going to a country where
Latin alone is used, and employed someone to teach you
Latin who spent his time trifling with you? I am sent to
prepare you for citizenship in heaven. Time is limited: I
must teach you the language of the heavenly Kingdom or
not converse with you at all (June 12, 1736). This was the
manner of association he desired with the group of at-
tractive young ladies whom he met March 13, 1736. One of
these was Sophia Christiana Hopkey, niece of a notable but
rather dishonorable official in whose home she stayed. She
was eighteen, fair and charming, and was apparently cap-

tivated by Wesley while courted by a crude fellow named Williamson. There were many private conferences with this apt pupil. She was really troubled, and wanted to escape by going to England. He presented religious arguments against this, and read to her from Law's *Serious Call*, from Ephrem Syrus and from Fleury's *History of the Church*—the last-mentioned, in order to show her examples of patience and martyrdom. When they were together on a boat trip and had to take shelter from the weather for the night, he saw by the firelight that she was awake. He remarked without approaching her and, he explains, without intending to say it: "Miss Sophy, I should think myself happy if I should spend my life with you." She burst into tears. He gives a fairly full and warmly appreciative description of Sophy, but adds:

> Such was the woman, according to my devout observation, of whom I now began to be much afraid. My desire and design still was to live single; but how long it would continue I knew not (November 1, 1736).

John Wesley's affairs of the heart were smothered by a belief that, at least for a man with a religious mission, celibacy was to be preferred to marriage. In 1743 he set forth this ascetic doctrine in *Thoughts on Marriage and a Single Life*, a tract which one Wesley authority says "might almost have been written by a convinced and ascetic Roman Catholic." But the question kept recurring. The same writer reminds us:

> He was thrice sick: at Georgia, in 1737, when Miss Hopkey nursed him; at Newcastle, in 1748, when Grace Murray nursed him; and in London, in 1761, when Mrs. Vazeille nursed him. And as a matter of fact Wesley wanted to marry each of his nurses in turn.[4]

Wesley had a will of steel, and he was later able to claim

[4] W. H. Fitchett, *Wesley and His Century* (Toronto: Briggs, 1908), pp. 456, 458–459.

that he had never proposed marriage to Sophy Hopkey. With Grace Murray it was different; but when he had found "scriptural reasons to marry," he lost confidence in Grace because of her fickleness and surrendered her to one of his preachers. On February 10, 1761, a sprained ankle exposed him to the nursing of a dangerous widow, Mrs. Vazeille. He married her on February 18. The marriage was in every way a mistake. On June 23, 1771, he writes in his Journal: "For what cause I know not, my wife set out for Newcastle, purposing 'never to return.' *Non eam reliqui; non dimisi; non revocabo.*" But she came back without his calling her; she came in repentance and left in anger several times thereafter until her death, which he records without emotion in 1781.

These matters would have been of great importance to most men, but in Wesley's case we must regard them as incidental and shedding only sidelights on his personality. Wesley had been rescued from the burning of his father's parsonage when he was ten years old, and his mother had taught him to think of himself as a brand plucked from the burning and elected for service to God. The sense of God was upon him, and he desired most of all to yield obedience to God. The first task was moral and spiritual self-improvement. Hence the elaborate program of prayer, the redoubled industry in study, the plans for "doing good to those that are hungry, naked, or sick," and to prisoners and unemployed tradesmen, that distinguished the Holy Club at Oxford, and the determination in Georgia to redeem the time with godly conversation.

Wesley met Indians in Georgia, but his desire to evangelize them was not encouraged either by the authorities or by his Savannah parishioners; the disturbed political state of the Indians themselves was also unfavorable. Everything now went against him. Sophy was married to Williamson.

Wesley had occasion to exclude her from communion. Causton, her uncle, attacked and prosecuted Wesley. We cannot follow the tale of defeat, full of strange incidents and private battles, recorded in the *Journal* to the time when Wesley "saw English land once more," January 29, 1738. Wesley returned to England beaten to his knees. He diagnosed the trouble thus: "I that went to America to convert others was never myself converted to God." He later annotated this with the words: "I am not sure of this"; in this afterthought he realized that he had been too severe on himself. Now he feels that his heart is "corrupt," that he is a "child of wrath" and that his own works are far from reconciling him to God. He lacks "that faith which St. Paul recommends to all the world" in Romans. He was nearer to that faith than he knew.

III

In his personal deflation Wesley acknowledges some benefits from the Georgia experience. He has found out what was in his heart. He has been delivered from youthful fears of the sea. He has come to know many of God's servants, particularly Moravians (February 3, 1738). Now in London begins his association with Peter Böhler, the Moravian leader. Böhler answered Wesley's doubts on whether he ought to preach, with the words, "Preach faith till you have it . . ." (March 4, 1738). Wesley began to expound, privately and publicly, the Pauline doctrine of faith. Böhler, he says later, "amazed me more and more by the account he gave of the fruits of living faith." Böhler left him confused by his notion of a sudden conversion—an "instantaneous work." Searching the Scriptures he found such conversions common in the primitive Church. But did they still happen? Böhler acquainted him with numerous living examples. A month before Wesley's conversion at the Aldersgate Street meeting, his *Journal* shows a complete intellectual acceptance of the pattern of faith which Böhler, a former Lutheran and now a Moravian, had lucidly explained to him; and he was frequently expressing it to individuals and congregations. The old Oxford company having now been scattered, John and Charles Wesley and others, under Böhler's influence, formed a new religious society at James Hutton's house in Fetter Lane, with a set of eleven rules which Wesley recites (May 1, 1738). But days follow in which he is "sorrowful and very heavy, being neither able to read, nor meditate, nor sing, nor pray, nor do anything." This depression lasts for two weeks. On the evening of May 24 the event happened which meant more than any other in his life.

That Wesley felt this to be the case at the time is manifest. He took the occasion to insert a short autobiographical statement recalling the religious stages through which he had come. He had hoped to be saved by the routines of religion. Thomas à Kempis (to whom without question he ascribes the *Imitatio Christi*) had given a new depth but had not changed this religious direction. From William Law's books "the light flowed in so mightily upon my soul, that everything appeared in a new view"; but this appears to mean only an intensification of his former earnestness to fulfill all righteousness. As noted in a previous chapter, he was to react strongly from Law's advice. He was vainly "active in outward works." In Savannah, he says, he was "beating the air." Then had come, through Böhler, the conviction of the necessity of renouncing all dependence upon works of righteousness.

On May 24 at 5 A.M. he read II Peter 1:4: "exceeding great and precious promises, even that ye should be partakers of the divine nature." That afternoon at St. Paul's he heard Purcell's anthem, "Out of the Deep." Then comes the most often quoted passage of the *Journal*, known by heart by every good Methodist:

> In the evening I went very unwillingly to a society in Aldersgate Street, where one was reading Luther's Preface to the *Epistle to the Romans*. About a quarter before nine, when he was describing the change which God works in the heart through faith in Christ, I found my heart strangely warmed. I felt I did trust in Christ, Christ alone, for salvation; and an assurance was given me that He had taken away *my* sin, even *mine*, and saved *me* from the law of sin and death (May 24, 1738).

The first effect was to set him praying with all his might for those who had despitefully used him. In the days following he had to fight off many temptations; now, however, he was not as before defeated by these but "always conqueror." He heard echoes of the anthem in St. Paul's; he quotes its comforting words two days afterwards: "My soul truly waiteth upon God . . . for God is our hope." The Luther text read at Aldersgate is needed to explain the narrative. Writers on Wesley have been very vague or clearly mistaken about Luther's Preface to *Romans* which Wesley says "one was reading." I have shown reason to believe that it was the translation of Luther's Preface to *Romans* made by one "W. W." from the enlarged Latin edition by Justus Jonas (1523), first printed in 1594 and reprinted in 1632.[5]

⁵ "Luther at Aldersgate," *London Quarterly and Holborn Review*, April, 1939, pp. 200–217. This article was finished some months before the appearance of R. Kissack's short study, "Wesley's Conversion, Text, Anthem and Homily," *Proceedings of the Wesley Historical Society*, Vol. XXII, Part I, March, 1939, pp. 1–6. Mr. Kissack thinks it more likely that it was the Latin text of this tract that was read, and cites the "*cor inflammat*" of the original as parallel to Wesley's "heart strangely warmed." W. W. uses the expressions: "the quickening Spirit and his lively impulsions and agitations in our heart"; "which Spirit doth make us new hearts, doth exhilarate us, doth excite and inflame our heart [for *cor inflammat*]; Faith . . . worketh mightily in our hearts"; "doth embolden the heart"; "work-

This is one of Luther's most eager statements of the doctrine of faith. It was paraphrased by Tyndale in that translator's preface to the epistle. The author is indeed exhilarated by his theme, faith and its fruits of good works:

He that doeth not his good works of such lively affection of the heart, is wholly in unbelief and a stranger and alien from the faith, as many of these be which in schools dispute and jangle. . . .

Faith before works is now the keynote of Wesley's testimony. In the *Journal* he tells of being in Oxford June 11, but omits to mention the sermon on salvation by faith which he preached that day in St. Mary's Church. In the sermon he expressly lauds Martin Luther's testimony to the doctrine discussed. He seems to have thought highly of this sermon: long afterwards he set it at the beginning of a collection of his *Works* (1771). Curnock's note on it is helpful but hardly brings out the force and boldness of this assertion of Reformation principles. A great deal of it Luther might have written. But the figures of speech and illustrations savor of Wesley's own experience. He refers to the prevalent immorality, spreading like a flood:

Can you empty the great deep drop by drop? Then you may reform us by dissuasives from particular vices. But let the righteousness which is of God by faith be brought in; and so shall its proud waves be stayed.

Wesley knew his debt to Luther and to the Moravian appropriation of Luther's teaching. But he was soon to be critical of the Moravians. Returning from a visit to their center at Herrnhut and to their leader, Zinzendorf (1738),

---

ing effectually in our hearts doth incyte and inflame us to do good." The English text was available, and I see no reason to suppose either that the members of the group as a whole would understand Latin or that the clumsy procedure of an oral translation following a Latin reading was employed. The assumption of some that most of those present were German-speaking Moravians is without foundation.

he wrote to the latter that there were "things he did not approve," and later he was to diverge from them more and more. He found them extolling faith in language strongly colored by antinomianism. When in June, 1741, he first read Luther's *Galatians* through, he somewhat unfairly found in this work the basis of Moravian antinomian mysticism (June 15, 1741). In 1749 Luther was still for him "a man highly favored of God and a blessed instrument in his hand," but it was regrettable that he had not had a frank friend to rebuke him for his bitter zeal (July 19, 1749). Wesley was sensitive to everything that put in jeopardy the basis of an active puritanic Christian ethic. The late Professor George Croft Cell was in a sound position in saying that Wesley was "essentially and thoroughly Puritan in his whole ethical outlook" and that in those aspects of the doctrine of justification which have to do with God's activity in human affairs he agrees with the Calvinist rather than with the Lutheran conception.[6] In a late sermon (No. XCVI) Wesley warns the Methodists that their sound belief in salvation by faith will not save them from hell hereafter if it fails now to save them from unholy tempers, pride, passion and peevishness. In his preaching he emphasized sanctification as the sequel to justification and insisted that it was not outward works but "an inward thing, namely the life of God in the soul of man" (September 13, 1739). Here he uses the phrase which formed the title of a little book by the Scottish mystic, Henry Scougall, which had helped Wesley in earlier days: *The Life of God in the Soul of Man.*[7]

[6] *The Rediscovery of John Wesley* (New York: Holt, 1935), pp. 152, 387.

[7] See Curnock, *op. cit.*, I, 169. Scougall was a brilliant Aberdeen scholar who died at the age of twenty-eight in 1679. His book appeared in numerous editions in Britain and America. It features the imitation of Christ in diligence, patience, charity and humility, and discourses on the "excellency of divine love."

IV

Wesley had now found himself, and he presently found his work. In April, 1739, he began "field preaching." Many churches had been closed to him but many people desired to hear him. He records a letter canceling a meeting as follows:

I received the following note:
Sir—our minister, having been informed that you are beside yourself, does not care you should preach in any of his churches. —I went however; and on Priestdown about half a mile from Pensford, preached Christ . . . (May 7, 1739).

Here Wesley lets us see how he became an itinerant outdoor preacher. He was charged with irregularity in invading other men's parishes. He sets down a letter written in reply to this charge after laying the matter "before the Lord." It is here that he says, serving notice on the world and the church,

I look upon all the world as my parish; thus far, I mean, that, in whatever part of it I am, I judge it meet, right, and my bounden duty to declare unto all that are willing to hear, the glad tidings of salvation. This is the work which I know God has called me to . . . (June 11, 1739).

Early in Wesley's itinerant ministry he tells us of a religiously crazed woman at Kingswood who sensed his approach three miles away: "Yonder comes Wesley," she screamed, "galloping as fast as he can" (October 27, 1739). A man who had the world for his parish would have to ride fast. But he did not force his horses to gallop. Nor did he like them slow and spiritless. Ordinarily his pace was a dog-trot. He had 250,000 miles to go by 1791, mostly on horseback. For years he averaged eight thousand miles a year, and the roads were generally bad. He has less to say than we would expect about his mounts. In normal conditions he gave them little attention. Like other travelers, he hired horses for the stages of his journey, and thus did not become attached to the individual beast. Men said that he was not an expert rider; but almost certainly they were men whom he outrode as far as distance is concerned. He has some interesting experiences with horses to record, and we may lighten our tale with a notice of two or three of these.

Once on a smooth road his horse "suddenly pitched upon his head and rolled over and over." Wesley suffered "a little bruise" (June 24, 1739). Two months later a collision occurred: "A person galloping swiftly rode full against me and overthrew man and horse, but without any hurt to either. Glory be to him that saveth man and beast!" (September 24, 1739). At another time his horse fell and, struggling to rise, fell again upon John Wesley. Some women providentially helped him into a house whose occupants responded to his religious message (October 25, 1741). A mishap could often be a spiritual opportunity. At Snowsfields:

the saddle slipping quite upon my mare's neck, I fell over her head, and she ran back into Smithfield. Some boys caught her and brought her to me again, cursing and swearing all the way. I spoke plainly to them, and they promised to amend. [But he had lost his saddle-cloth, and there was more swearing while other helpers put it on.] I turned to one and the other and spoke in love. They all took it well and thanked me much. I gave them two or three little books which they promised to read over carefully (August 22, 1743).

Another horse meeting a cart in a narrow alley halted suddenly and shot Wesley over his head "like an arrow." Again he tells us:

On my return [to Gainsborough] my mare, rushing violently through a gate, struck my heel against the gate-post and left me behind her in an instant, laid on my back at full length. She stood still till I rose and mounted again; and neither of us was hurt at all (March 8, 1764).

Once in Ireland he rode ninety miles in one midsummer day, using up one horse and obtaining a second in the afternoon. At 11 P.M. he was turned away from an inn; the good woman opened the door but only far enough "to let out four dogs upon me," so he had to ride till midnight (June 15, 1750). These were no doubt the typical hazards of a life on horseback. Wesley seems to have had his full share of such mishaps. But he thought himself especially immune to the stumbling of his mounts, and in 1770 he takes time to explain this:

Near thirty years ago I was thinking: How is it that no horse ever stumbles while I am reading? (History, poetry and philosophy I commonly read on horseback, having other employment at other times.) No account can possibly be given but this: because then I throw the reins on his neck. In riding above a hundred thousand miles, I scarce ever remember any horse (except two that would fall head over heels anyway) to fall or make a considerable stumble while I rode *with a slack rein* (March 28, 1770).

We might call this the slack-rein, or *laissez-faire*, method of horsemanship! The horses probably liked it; but let us not suppose that the rider was mentally relaxed. For example: "In riding to Rosmead [Ireland] I read Sir John Davis's *Historical Relations concerning Ireland*." He reviews the book in six short paragraphs (April 21, 1760). It would appear that we have not advanced very far: you cannot drive an automobile and read "history, poetry and philosophy." In later years, with better roads and stagecoaches, Wesley traveled mostly on wheels, with others driving, and was then able to write as well as read on his way. But sometimes he ceased his travels for a few weeks to write for the press. On one of these occasions he observes: "In my hours of walking

I read Dr. Calamy's 'Abridgment of Mr. Baxter's Life' "
(April 3, 1754). Wesley had once written to his mother
from Oxford, "Leisure and I have parted company," and
they were never to meet again.[8] Wesley did not found and
organize the Methodists from an office chair. Sometimes he
finds the stagecoach too slow. On his way from Chatham to
London in 1778, the old man left the coach when it was delayed, to walk up the hill ahead. He walked five miles before
it overtook him, and enjoyed it: "The more I walk the better I sleep," is his comment (November 5, 1778).

The pace he set was exacting. His little body was well
knit and strong, but he often felt the strain. Having preached
thirty times in eleven days and attended various meetings of
his groups, he remarks: "I find myself a little exhausted"
(September 22, 1760). In 1753 he was greatly troubled by
a cough and fever. Not knowing whether he would live or
die, and in order "to prevent vile panegyric," he wrote an
epitaph to be used if needed: "Here lieth the body of John
Wesley, a brand plucked from the burning; who died of a
consumption in the fifty-first year of his age, not leaving,
after his debts are paid, ten pounds behind him . . ." (November 26, 1753). His illness continuing for months, he took
the opportunity to write a book, his *Notes on the New Testament*, and was soon able to preach again (March 26, 1754).

His travels brought him to strange sleeping rooms. At Mel-
larbarn, in a mining district, he reports cheerfully:

> My lodging was not such as I should have chosen, but what
> Providence chooses is always good. My bed was considerably
> underground. . . . The closeness was more troublesome to me at

[8] Wesley and Dr. Samuel Johnson had a liking for each other,
and Wesley visited Johnson on his deathbed (1784). Boswell reports
(as of March 31–April 2, 1778) this remark of Johnson: "John Wesley's conversation is good, but he is never at leisure. He is always
obliged to go at a certain hour. This is very disagreeable to a man
who loves to fold his legs and have out his talk, as I do."

first than the coolness; but I let in a little fresh air by breaking a pane of paper . . . in the window, and then slept sound till morning (June 9, 1752).

He had to face a good deal of violent opposition. At Wednesbury near Birmingham after he had preached, an angry mob clamored to get hold of his person. They took him to another town, and aroused a sleeping magistrate to try him for his psalm singing and early rising. The magistrate dismissed them. Fifty men undertook to convoy him back, but another mob snatched him from them. In course of what followed a woman defending Wesley knocked down three or four men. Seeing his steadfast courage, one of the mob changed his attitude and said: "Sir, I will spend my life for you." In the end he was safely brought back to his praying friends (October 20, 1743). At Scotter near his early home at Epworth, his preaching was the occasion of "continual riots" which were, however, quelled by "an upright magistrate" (April 2, 1764). "I came to Leeds," he writes in 1745, "preached at five and at eight met the society; after which the mob pelted us with dirt and stones" (September 12, 1745). At Plymouth in 1747, "perceiving the violence of the rabble still increasing, I walked down into the thickest of them, and took the captain of the mob by the hand. He immediately said, 'Sir, I will see you safe home' " and offered to knock down anybody who touched Wesley. He was "a very tall man," and with meaningful glances back at the crowd, he convoyed the little missioner to a friendly door (June 27, 1747). Wesley's chosen policy was "to look a mob in the face," but sometimes friends whisked him away when he would have done this (August 6, 1746). Here is another typical experience:

In the evening as I was preaching in St. Ives, Satan began to fight for his kingdom. The mob of the town burst into the room and created much disturbance, roaring and striking those that stood in their way as though Legion himself possessed them. I would fain have persuaded our people to stand still; but the zeal of some and the fear of others had no ears: so that, finding the uproar increase, I went into the midst, and brought the head of the mob up with me to the desk. I received but one blow on the side of the head; after which we reasoned the case, till he grew milder and milder, and at length undertook to quiet his companions (September 16, 1743).

This was a rough life for the fastidious son of a rectory who hated everything untidy. His descriptions of persons are often vivid and vigorous. In a stormy night on the Irish Sea he grew "tired of staying on deck" in the wind and rain:

But we met another storm below: for who should be there but the famous Mr. Gr..... of Carnarvonshire—a clumsy, overgrown, hard-faced man; whose countenance I could only compare to that (which I saw at Drury Lane thirty years ago) of one of the ruffians in "Macbeth."

We note how long Wesley remembered the face of an actor whose appearance on the stage was for minutes only. This passenger poured forth "a volley of ribaldry, obscenity and blasphemy" to surpass the language of Billingsgate (March 25, 1750). There are many such picturesque ruffians and they are usually (as in this case) drunk.

In some instances the character sketches are whimsical, as in the case of this Irishman:

I talked with a warm man, who was always very zealous for the Church when he was very drunk, and just able to stammer out the Irish proverb, "No gown, no crown." He was quickly convinced that, whatever we were, he was himself a child of the devil. We left him full of good resolutions, which held several days (March 23, 1748).

At Newark as late as 1780 Wesley notes, with amusement and a suitable classical reference, the case of "one big man exceeding drunk" whose wife seized him by the collar, boxed his ears repeatedly and "dragged him away like a calf" (June 12, 1780). He records without comment talking on one occasion with a man "who at the advice of his pastor, had, very calmly and deliberately beat his wife with a large stick till she was black and blue almost from head to foot." This conscientious wife beater "insisted it was his duty to do so, because she was surly and ill-natured; and that he was full of faith all the time he was doing it, and had been ever since" (May 28, 1757).

Wesley, however, sometimes came into cultured homes of the nobility. Here is a characteristic report of such:

I spent an hour agreeably and profitably with Lady G..... H..... and Sir C..... H..... It is well a few rich and noble are called. O, that God would increase their number! But I should rejoice (were it the will of God) if it were done by the ministry of others. If I might choose, I should still (as I have done hitherto) preach the Gospel to the poor (November 17, 1759).

The reader will note the fundamental contrast here of Wesley's ministry with that of William Law. Near Templemacateer, Ireland, he notes his maladjustment in scenes of wealth and ease:

Being at ease and in honor in a gentleman's house, I found little life or power. I could not bear to stay in this place; all things are so pretty and convenient. About twelve we took horse. (Additions, in Curnock, *op. cit.*, VIII, 154. April 2, 1748.)

But sometimes Wesley was mildly astonished by the response even of the rich to his preaching, as once in Newcastle:

On Monday the 20th a great part of the congregation (which filled the room) were some of the finest people I had ever seen there. Surely God is working a new thing in the earth. Even to the rich is the Gospel preached! And there are, of these also,

who have ears to hear and hearts to receive the truth as it is in
Jesus (April 20, 1747).

V

Wesley paid many visits to Scotland and Ireland. In both
these countries many things were strange to him, but this
fact did not make his experiences the less enjoyable. His
satisfaction with his work in Scotland was limited, however,
by the limitations of its success. The Scots, as a rule, were
trained and critical listeners to sermons, quite unlike the
largely unchurched masses who ardently hated and loved
his messages in England. Toward Wesley they were neither
cold nor hot; he rejoiced when they exhibited even a little
warmth. In the *Journal* he has recorded, in his cursory way,
some penetrating critical judgments of Scottish Presbyterian
religious habits. While in Georgia he visited a Highland
Scottish Presbyterian community and made this comment:

I was surprised to hear an extempore prayer before a written
sermon. Are not the words we speak to God to be set in order
at least as carefully as those we speak to our fellow worms?
(January 2, 1737)

Long years afterwards in Glasgow on a Friday the congregation was "miserably small." "The Scots," says Wesley,
"love the Word of the Lord on the Lord's day" (May 28,
1790). "This is a nation swift to hear, slow to speak, but not
slow to wrath," he wrote when he had ridden from Aberdeen to Inverness (June 7, 1764). At Nairn he observes:
"Everyone here (in North Britain) at least loves to hear the
word of God" (June 11, 1764). He much preferred the
Anglican to the Scottish communion service. But in the Episcopal Church at Aberdeen the reader was so inaudible that
Wesley thinks it would be better to pay him for doing nothing than for doing mischief (May 31, 1772). We may say, I

think, that Wesley remained a little puzzled by the regular churchgoing Scots. He often remarks on their devout attention in church, their willingness to hear even the most cutting words and their lack of emotional response. "I know of none like them for bearing plain dealing" (August 4, 1787). "I admire this people, so decent, so serious, so perfectly unconcerned." They are "the best hearers in Europe" (May 12, 1788). Wesley paid a number of visits to the General Assembly of the Church of Scotland. He failed to see in it that dignity of procedure that Whitefield praised. He seems to have disapproved of the admission of the public to its deliberations. On one occasion he witnessed with annoyance a five-hour debate in the assembly on the weighty question: "Shall Mr. Lindsay be moved to Kilmarnock?" (May 28, 1764). It is not apparent that he understood the tension in the Scottish Church between the minority who resented and the majority who acquiesced in the injurious Patronage Act of Queen Anne's time.

VI

Wesley had been a thorough student and, despite the handicaps of a traveler's life, he continued to be a reader of current and older books. He rarely mentions a work he has read without halting for a terse comment. More often than not his judgments are sharply critical. His severest remarks are on books alien to traditional Christian teaching. In his Georgia period he spent some days reading alternately Bishop Patrick on prayer and the works of "Machiavel." He made careful notes on the latter and concluded that, in comparison with a prince who would follow Machiavelli's model, "Domitian or Nero would be an angel of light" (January 27–29, 1737). On reading *Émile* he pronounced Rousseau a "consummate coxcomb," adding that "his brother

infidel," Voltaire, was "well-nigh as great a coxcomb."
Rousseau's statement that young children never love old
people he thought patently false and silly: not only do they
love their grandparents, but "they love all who love them"
(February 3, 1770). Wesley is wary of speculative or mystical books. Thus the *German Theology* seems to him a
work of "affected obscurity" (November 12, 1741), and
Swedenborg, an "entertaining madman" (February 28,
1770).

He is inclined to be more skeptical of historical works
that feature marvelous incidents than of contemporary tales
of the supernatural. What he asks of historians is a just and
critical judgment: but at some points his own historical par-
tisanship—for example, his view that Mary of Scotland was
"one of the most blameless of women"—weights his opinion
of an author. There is a refreshing directness in his estimates of historical writers. Eusebius, the Church historian,
is "a weak, credulous, and thoroughly injudicious writer"
(December 19, 1741). Knox's *History of the Reformation
within the Realm of Scotland* prompts the observation that
God used, to reform the Church, some "sour, overbearing
and passionate men"—not because of these qualities, but despite them (June 23, 1766). The famous *History of Charles
the Fifth* by the Scottish Church leader and historian, William Robertson, disappointed him greatly. The book is introduced by a long study of medieval Europe, in which
Wesley seems to have got bogged down. "Where," he asks,
"is Charles the fifth?" (April 28, 1772). His statement that
it might as well be a history of Alexander the Great ignores
three-quarters of the book and raises a question about the
thoroughness of his reading on journey.

Some books, evidently, he did read carefully. It is interesting to find that he read with deep appreciation the play,
Douglas, by the Reverend John Home, which shocked the

Kirk so gravely as to produce a serious controversy. Wesley was "astonished to find it one of the finest tragedies I ever read," but thought that some lines (presumably those regarded by Home's critics as offensive to religious taste) should have been omitted, and that it should not have been staged in Edinburgh. Many books, of course, were sympathetically read by Wesley, and some of them he permitted to change his views of important matters. For example, his reading of Lord King's *Primitive Church* (May 20, 1746) permanently altered his conception of the ministry and made it possible for him, long afterwards, to take the bold measure of ordaining ministers for American Methodism. In a letter of September 10, 1784, justifying this course of action, he notes: "Lord King's account of the Primitive Church convinced me many years ago, that bishops and presbyters are the same order, and consequently have the same right to ordain."

VII

It may have been in some degree the experiences of violence in his early ministry that made Wesley always a close observer of the behavior of congregations and throngs. He compares one community with another in this respect, and the same community on succeeding visits. Often he compares Scottish and Irish with English congregations. Usually the Scots are more respectful and less responsive than the English. But as early as 1748 he takes the older English preaching places as models of good conduct. Often he had no idea what sort of reception he would receive. At Oxmantown in Ireland he notes: "We expected noise, but there was none; the whole congregation was as quiet and still as that in Bristol or London" (March 20, 1748). Visiting Birmingham in 1761 he refers to an unrecorded earlier experience there in the words: "The last time I was in Birmingham the stones flew on every side. If any disturbance were made now, the disturber would be in greater danger than the preacher" (May 31, 1761). We find many such statements as these: "At five I preached to an exceedingly well-behaved congregation." "The people did not come close to me, but stood in a half-moon some yards off, leaving a considerable space in the midst. The very children behaved with remarkable seriousness." "The whole multitude was silent while I was speaking. Not a whisper was heard; but the moment I had done the chain fell off their tongues. I was really surprised. Surely never was such a cackling made on the banks of the Cayster . . ." (an allusion to a passage in Pope's translation of the *Iliad*). "It rained the whole time I was preaching, but the congregation regarded it no more than I did." "Notwithstanding the rain, every man, woman and child stayed to the end." "It rained all the time I was walking to the Green . . . but the moment I began to preach the rain ceased."

The climate of the British Isles, in all its moods, is reflected in Wesley's vivid phrases throughout the *Journal*. Take for example the contrast of these two extracts, not far apart:

I rode to Cradley. Here also the multitude of people obliged me to stand abroad [out of doors], although the north wind whistled round my head. About one I took the field again at Stowbridge. Many of the hearers were wild as colts untamed; but the bridle was in their mouths. At six I began at Dudley. The air was as cold as I had ever felt. But I trust God warmed many hearts (March 19, 1770).

I preached at six at Dawgreen near Dewsbury. All things contributed to make it a refreshing season; the gently-declining sun, the stillness of the evening, the beauty of the meadows, and fields through which "the smooth clear river drew his sinuous train," the opposite hills and woods, and the earnestness of the people, covering the top of the hill on which we stood; and above all, the day-spring from on high, the consolation of the Holy One (July 5, 1770).

In many instances he presents scenes of sunshine and smiling beauty. But it is not his habit to linger sentimentally upon these. (The eighteenth century's favorite word "sentimental" he calls, with special reference to Sterne's *Sentimental Journey*, a "nonsensical word"—February 11, 1772.) Nor will he permit the romanticizing of rural life. Quoting Horace in a passage lauding the countryman's beans and bacon, he asks: "Was Horace in his senses when he talked thus, or the servile herd of his imitators?" (November 5, 1766.) In contrast he sympathetically enumerates the farmer's hard tasks. The weather showed the great evangelist no favors, and he asked for none. When it was stormy he was perhaps a little proud of his ability to take it. To surrender and adjourn to a room usually meant that he would have to speak to a much reduced number of hearers; but this was sometimes unavoidable.

VIII

Like most people of his time, Wesley was a little credulous of supernatural phenomena. He has many observations on witchcraft and apparitions. He defends belief in witchcraft: it is infidels who have "hooted it out of the world" (July 1, 1770). He introduces the story of the strange case of Elizabeth Hobson with the admission that he never himself has seen an apparition; nor has he seen a murder, yet he believes there are such things (May 25, 1765). He observes with puzzled interest and describes in detail the unaccountable symptoms of a number of children in Brechin who, in strange seizures that he thought preternatural, ran, leaped, climbed to rooftops and leaned backward without falling (June 1, 1764). He gives space to the reports of apparitions of dead persons attested by Sarah Maitland "on whose veracity I could depend" (October 8, 1775).

Another interest lies in his ideas of medicine and his ready assumption of the role of physician in many cases. He had great confidence in his prescriptions; very little confidence in the medical profession. "I rescued her from death and the doctors," he says of a child supposed to be dying of smallpox (January 7, 1773). It was through his desire to advance the art of healing that he came to be deeply interested in electricity. He provided stations for the electrification treatment of a variety of diseases, and reports in 1757 that hundreds, perhaps thousands, have greatly benefited by these treatments (November 9, 1757). He once found a man suffering great pain which doctors had diagnosed as "gout of the stomach." Wesley said, citing two medical works, that it was angina pectoris, and that the patient must be "electrified." This was done and the sufferer was thereby relieved and slept comfortably (April 19, 1774). When between York and Tadcaster the chaise in which Wesley was traveling broke down, he tells us: "I borrowed a horse, but as he was none of the easiest, in riding three miles I was so thoroughly electrified that the pain in my breast was quite cured" (May 14, 1777).

Wesley's conversation was almost constantly religious; but a good deal of his reading was in nonreligious fields, and he had other secular interests. The *Journal* is not very valuable for his politics. It does reveal to us his keen observation of nature, his love of well-tended gardens and his interest in curiosities and freaks of nature. Within a year of his death he goes to see the "monster" on exhibit at the Tower, which he concludes is half bear and half boar, and gives a good description of the pelicans observed on the same occasion (September 16, 1790). Twenty-five years earlier, having found a lion in Edinburgh that showed a fondness for music, he visited the lions in the Tower, accompanied by one who played the German flute. The result was inconclusive. One of a group of four or five lions came forward showing pleasure, while a tiger became greatly excited, leaping over and dodging under the lion. Wesley, who is looking for some profound law behind the phenomena, finds it all inexplicable (December 31, 1764).

With advancing age, until he had passed fourscore, Wesley's health improved. At eighty-one in Scotland, "to ease the horses" he left them behind at Nairn, walked twelve and one-half miles through heavy rain to Inverness and there preached to a large congregation (May 10, 1784). Six weeks later he was at Epworth, his birthplace, where he set down these words:

I am as strong at eighty-one as I was at twenty-one, but abundantly more healthy, being a stranger to the headache, toothache and other bodily disorders which attended me in my youth (June 28, 1784).

At eighty-five he notes "the gentle steps whereby age steals upon us": his sight is slowly failing (December 15, 1788). In the upper decades he frequently ascribes his continued vigor to the goodness of God, and secondarily to his habits of early rising, early preaching and constant travel. We find really passionate appeals for early rising: late risers were from his viewpoint in a parlous state! (April 5, 1774.)

IX

John Wesley's *Journal* is one of the most fascinating of historical records of life in Britain and Ireland for any period, and especially in England, whose folk he best understood. It reveals in unvarnished realism the dangerous substratum of barbarism in eighteenth-century society, the helpless starvation of the destitute, the filth and misery of the jails, the ignorance and suspicion of the working classes, the roads, muddy but improving through the years. Wesley moves over these highways and byways with such haste and joy of movement that we fail to realize their length and weariness. For the King's business required haste. Men were perishing for the message which a merciful God had placed upon his lips.

Even to the secular mind the *Journal* is priceless; but virtually everything in it is set in the light of a religious interpretation of life. Something of the endless variety of material in the *Journal* has been suggested by what we have been saying. It is needful to be aware that the great record has not only variety but also unity. It is a complete unity, derived from the author's unreserved consecration to one task. Essentially the task was to communicate to needy souls the Gospel by which they might be saved. But it involved far more than an impersonal proclamation. Wesley solicitously piloted inquirers and converts as they broke from the bondage and futility of an irreligious life and entered on a course of the purposeful cultivation of holiness. Whether he addressed an assembly of thousands or talked urgently with an individual, his theme was salvation, his aim the regeneration of sinners. The unabated zeal with which he pursued his mission year by year was fed by convincing evidence that an amazing change took place in countless hearers. Wesley does not show elation at his own power of eloquence. But he could not be unaware that his message was effective in an unprecedented way:

> We came to Hainton after sunset. I never saw so large a congregation here. I declared to them all (Protestants and Papists) "the grace of our Lord Jesus Christ," and they seemed to be indeed, as Homer says, ἔπεα πτερόεντα, "winged words" that flew as arrows from the hands of the Most High to the heart of every hearer (Feb. 24, 1747).

Common enough are entries of this sort:

I rode to Liverpool, where also was such a work of God as had never been known there before. We had a surprizing congregation in the evening, and, as it seemed, all athirst for God (August 2, 1762).

Not less common are his little case reports on individuals at various stages of religious stimulation. "I talked with J . . . . . D . . . . . , a gentleman's coachman, an uncommon monument of mercy . . . ," but as yet unstable. Any relaxation of effort would have been desertion of those "athirst for God" and of coachmen and others who were "monuments of mercy." This is the book of a saint, whose devotion was not the less complete for lack of protracted contemplation. He was often in prayer; but the impression conveyed by this record is that of a sustained spiritual exhilaration in ceaseless activity.